Bryan Dietrich is my favorite mystic. I'... relationship to the divine is more medium than scholar. He invites it all in: the ancient and numinous, the postmodern and spandex clad. Then, like the ecstatic Theresa, the man-woman-man Tiresias, he speaks: earthy, oracular, earnest. Super. Wonder. Wow.

—MARTA FERGUSON, *Mustang Sally Pays Her Debt to Wilson Pickett*

Imagine the guy who owned the local comic book store was also a top-notch poet, and you begin to get at the level of intelligence and depth Dietrich brings to this collection. Imagine that guy also had the ear of Hopkins, Larkin, or Muldoon. These are smart, funny, well-informed poems, and after you'll never look at Superman and Wonder Woman the same.

—KEVIN RABAS, *All That Jazz*

Bryan Dietrich has established himself as the inimitable leader of the exploration of heroic tropes via poetry. Not since Joseph Campbell has the hero been laid so bare, hurt so badly, and loved so deeply.

—JASON MOTT, *The Returned*

Single Bound is a very soulful double collection about the glamour and terrors of being truly singular. Without equal. Utterly alone. What's so fresh and essential about Bryan Dietrich's take on the Superman and Wonder Woman characters, both of whom he so "gets," is that it skips the loud civic heroics and the messy private lives of these fantastically well-known subjects, passes over the stuff of comic books and movies, in favor of the artfully quiet and secret stuff. These poems are transporting, pulsing with mystery and wit, eros and empathy; and they're formally beautiful too.

—TOM DE HAVEN, *It's Superman!*

Bryan Dietrich never fails to delight on each page of *Single Bound.* His discoveries and insights into the personas of superheroes are deeply felt and intellectually satisfying.

—JEANNINE HALL GAILEY, *Field Guide to the End of the World*

In *Single Bound* Bryan Dietrich shows us a poet in his height, presenting a coherent and ambitious vision, challenging our sense of verse and modern myth-making. Reimagining yet consistent within the established mythology of the iconic figures of Superman and Wonder Woman, Dietrich takes us on a journey grounded in both humanity and super-humanity, probing what it means to be alien in the world of men. From the "Secret Diaries of Lois Lane" and "www.amazon.com" to "Several Stories, Single Bound" Dietrich's engaging wit and incisive observations will reshape your look at the potential of these seemingly immutable figures of pop culture. Global, cosmic, humane, and breathtaking, read this collection and wonder!

—BRYAN THAO WORRA, *Demonstra*

The biggest struggles don't come in tights. This is the crux of Bryan Dietrich's *Single Bound.* Dietrich uses a masterful combination of forms and personas to offer a multifaceted and multidimensional examination of the two most important American superheroes. But, just like the best superhero stories aren't only about superheroes, this collection is not only about Superman and Wonder Woman. It is not only about Clark Kent and Diana Prince. Humanity sits at the core of *Single Bound.* In his depiction of these fictional saviors, Dietrich makes us question why humanity wants a savior and, most importantly, why humanity deserves to be saved.

—JASON MCCALL, *Dear Hero*

Bryan Dietrich is some kind of Hermes, transgressing, as he does, all those bounded boundaries in order to mercurially map the *terra incognito* of tectonic wonder. Think of these souped-up sequences as accumulations of armor-plated, hefty zeppelin thought balloons brooding overhead, equipped with ecstatic cloud-to-cloud lightning, which will never, ever dissipate. These mythic verses are brilliant billboards composed of refracting stars, cursively sky-written, chiseled into the solid blue yonder of severely clear and clairvoyant skies.

—MICHAEL MARTONE, *Winesburg, Indiana*

SINGLE BOUND

SINGLE BOUND

KRYPTON NIGHTS / AMAZON DAYS

BRYAN D. DIETRICH

WordFarm
SEATTLE, WASHINGTON

WordFarm
334 Lakeside Ave S, #207
Seattle, WA 98144
www.wordfarm.net
info@wordfarm.net

USA ISBN-13: 978-1-60226-018-4
USA ISBN-10: 1-60226-018-4
Printed in the United States of America
Cover Design: Andrew Craft
First Edition: 2018

Library of Congress Cataloguing-in-Publication Data

Names: Dietrich, Bryan D. author.
Title: Single bound / Bryan D. Dietrich.
Description: First edition. | Seattle, Washington : WordFarm, 2018. |
    Includes bibliographical references and index. |
Identifiers: LCCN 2017056909 (print) | LCCN 2017060667 (ebook) |
    ISBN 9781602264250 (ebook) | ISBN 1602264252 (ebook) |
    ISBN 9781602260184 (pbk.: alk. paper)
Classification: LCC PS3604.I37 (ebook) | LCC PS3604.I37 A6 2018
(print) | DDC 811/.6–dc23

LC record available at https://lccn.loc.gov/2017056909

P 10 9 8 7 6 5 4 3 2 1
Y 22 21 20 19 18

Acknowledgments

I would like to thank the following journals in which some of these poems have appeared:

KRYPTON NIGHTS

The Paris Review:	"The Fourth Man in the Fire"
	"The Trials of Job"
	"The Theft of the Firstborn"
	"The Letter of the Law"
	"The Face of the Deep"
	"The Destruction of the Temple"
	"Behold the Man"
	The Model"
Prairie Schooner:	"Man or Superman"
	"Orgasm Over Mt. Ararat"
The Nation:	"Give to Her Your Cloak Also"
Quarterly West:	"The End of Days"
	"Krypton Nights"
	"On Jephthah"
	"The Else"
	"JHVH"
	"The Mysteries of Azazel"
	"The Curse of the Pharaohs"
The Bellingham Review:	"Through a Glass, Darkly"

Thanks to Writers at Work and Albert Goldbarth for awarding "The Jor-El Tapes" the 1996 Writers at Work Fellowship in Poetry. Thanks also to Linda Gregerson, Carl Phillips, Marie Ponsot, Grace Schulman, *The Nation,* and the 92nd Street Y for awarding "Autobiography of a Cape" and "The Lois Lane Diaries" the 2001 "Discovery"/*The Nation* Award in Poetry. Finally, thanks to Richard Howard and Zoo Press for awarding *Krypton Nights* the 2001 *Paris Review* Poetry Prize.

American Poets Against the War	"Lies"
Cliterature	"The Breath of Life"
Dissections	"Sacred Sites"
Drawn to Marvel	"Superman's *Other* Secret" (reprint)
Farrago's Wainscot	"W.W.F."
	"W.W.J.D."
	"Several Stories, Single Bound"
Licking River Review	"The Seduction of the Innocent"
	"www.amazon.com"
	"Discipline & Punish"
	"WWII"
	"The Dynamo and the Virgin"
	"The Text"
Mayo Review	"Paradise Island"
	"Utopia"
	"Essay on Man"
	"Common Sense"
	"Vindication of the Rights of Woman"
	"The Rights of Man"
	"The Second Sex"
	"The Prince"
Missouri Review	"I, Wonder"
	"Phaedrus"
	"Everyman"
	"The Feminine Mystique"
	"From Ritual to Romance"
	"Allegory of the Cave"
	"Leviathan"
	"The Descent of Woman"
	"Superman's *Other* Secret"

Special thanks to the Book Rack where I traded my first comics and to my father who took me there; to Mrs. Woods who introduced me to myth and to Jimmy and Duane who helped me name all the plants in her class after the JLA; to Moench and Buscema whose *Warriors of the Shadow Realm* made me want to make my own comics; to Marston, Peter, Gaines, and DC who reinvented Wonder; to Lynda Carter who gave that wonder shape; to Terry, Bobby, Jeff, and Memphis Comics who infected me with the urge to collect; to Miller and Daniels and Prairie Dog Comics who gave me an excuse to "do research"; to Nick, my son, who has reminded me why I love literature in three colors; to Chris who takes credit for everything cool herein; and to Gina, the Amazon I asked to marry me atop the Empire State Building in MMII.

For Gina Greenway,
Paradise

Contents

BOOK II: AMAZON DAYS

THE DEATH OF THE AUTHOR

S/W

BOOK ONE
KRYPTON NIGHTS

He thought according to the Law, spoke according to the Law,
and did according to the Law; so that he was the holiest in all
the living world, the best ruling in exercising rule, the brightest
in brightness, and most glorious in glory, the most victorious in
victory. And at his sight the demons rushed away.

—ZOROASTER
The Zend-Avesta, 591 B.C.E.

Superman never made any money
For saving the world from Solomon Grundy
And sometimes I despair the world will never see
Another man like him

—CRASH TEST DUMMIES
The Ghosts That Haunt Me, 1991

I, KENT

Listen, it isn't even my planet.
I just work here. A man of letters, mild
mannered, nerves of less than steel. Yes, I can
outrun most anything—thieves, mid-range sports
sedans, Shoemaker-Levy—can chew
a mouthful of coal to a cud of diamonds,
but I'm not as Delphic as you dream. I get
sleep apnea, hemorrhoids, runs in my tights.

I like *Gilligan's Island* and late night horror
flick medleys. Thermonuclear trust funds,
Greenpeace for guns, heavy metal milk lobbyists . . .
None of it gets me wet the way it used to.
If I could, I'd curl up in my cape
with an old comic, an orange soda,
a little Vivaldi. No telephone
booths; just Ming the Merciless to take me

away. Oh well. Shit happens. Worlds collide,
babes fall out of the sky, grow up, get lives.
My flat's just over there. No, the brownstone.
Yeah, that one. Corner room, third from— No. Up, up . . .
Anyway, I took this position because,
frankly, it looked like a job for me. Now
I'm not so sure anymore. I'm tired of being,
well, necessary. You don't know what it's like.

Hardly feeling a thing, seeing through
people, overhearing assassination plots

two countries over and still needing
new underwear every Christmas. One day
I hate the boots, belt, bikini, this *S* appliqué;
the next, I feel like punching every hornrimmed
dweeb I see. Dad warned me it might be like this.
"Son," he said, "you'll just wanna come home." Problem is,

I can't.

AUTOBIOGRAPHY OF A CAPE

A Crown of Sonnets by C. Kent

"Fair enough." Perry came around from behind his desk.
"We all have a life outside these walls, and what you do with
yours is none of my damn business . . . as long as it doesn't
reflect badly on the Planet."

—ROGER STERN
The Death and Life of Superman, 1993

I. THE FOURTH MAN IN THE FIRE

Home from a hard day's Armageddon,
slipping out of spandex and into spectacles,
from one high life bold above the abandon
into another (shall we say less Pericles

than Prospero), I find that I suspect
this Superman I've become. Dressing down
is easier, the lie somehow less circumspect.
And though this *too* is dressing up, the clown

suit *cum* reporter's wardrobe boasts less blood
between the seams. I don't mind the dumbing
down, really. Being the neighborhood
god, all guts and gusto, well, it's numbing.

But here, just another byline for a vast news magnate,
I can stumble, fumble, fail. I can always quit the *Planet*.

II. THE TRIALS OF JOB

I could stumble, fumble, fail, quit the planet,
head for the first unrehearsed star to the right
and then vanish, over lunch, say, some strange event
horizon. My alibi? Space frenzy. Airtight.

But, approaching omnipotence, where does one run?
I suppose I just feel torn sometimes, between
cape and capacity, between what I've done
and what you've *let* me do. The half seen

gestures of this politico, that pontiff,
the anchor's sly nod at half a hundred stations,
editors, my boss (most people, really, if
you want to know the truth), they, their nations,

whole parliaments have ratified me.
What happens, then, should I turn? Back toward eternity?

III. THE THEFT OF THE FIRSTBORN

What happens then? Should I return, back toward
eternity? Start over, seek that old crabgrass orchard
deep in the Kansas scree and wait for my metal
cradle, the star that chose Pa's field, to settle?

Actually, it was all corn where my crib
came down, but if I *could* go back, trace time's rib
around to come out thirty years more whole
than any toddler, ostensibly, set before me; if I stole

myself from then, left only a smoking husk
behind; if I raised myself on some dead, dusk-
less world, that violet-blue one just off the edge of M31,
how, then, would I explain this suit to my "son"?

How define crest? How, without wars, Czars, rules?
On a field, yellow, the letter *S,* gules?

IV. THE LETTER OF THE LAW

On a field of yellow, the letter *S*, gules.
This is how my parents found me, flames
cutting a swath across the farm road near the school's,
only stopping their red weave where the James'

property ended and Pa's began. The sign
my folks followed, then—that cosmic spoor
which led to a small, blue craft cratered to the spine—
spelled not so much a warning as the future.

When my mother—unaware of the root
of her design, that red, ruthless curve—stitched
something less letter than Kansas cornfield
to my chest, anchored me to my past, affixed

me to an arc dark as blood, was it heraldry or shield?
She and Pa still read the sky. I've tried to follow suit.

V. THE FACE OF THE DEEP

My folks still read the sky I've tried to follow. The suit,
though, gets in the way of being human.
Even *being* human, stubbing one's foot,
say, or regretting the blood-letting of all but a few . . . Man,

it's rough. There are times I've had to reset teeth, back
into laws I've broken myself, ensuring
some purer notion. Two selves then. Each a plank
for the other's platform; each, a hasty mooring.

Like some deranged Phoenician navigator
set adrift on theory molded mostly of the paper
he's penned his calculations on, I guess I find my taste
for figures growing thin. And how odd to waste

time hanging sky, when I'd rather be down
here anyway. Deep, where Superman may drown.

VI. THE DESTRUCTION OF THE TEMPLE

Here, anywhere, deep. Where Superman would drown.
Why even ask? Of course that would be untimely
for us both. So maybe I step into a ray gun,
one of Luthor's, burn away the steel. Finally

farm myself out to a sun that doesn't heal
so well. Or, what the hey, go ahead and steal
one of those Green Lantern rings, wish myself
no longer bird but plain. The thing is, your health

has depended on me, this antibody,
too long. And you would, I suspect, *still* see
me, bring me back like some dead, desert King,
refit me in his sequins. No, nothing

I can do, then, will relinquish me my cup.
These days I flee to where the ice is calving, cracking up.

VII. BEHOLD THE MAN

These days I flee to where the ice is calving.
Where cracking up comes easier on reflection
of each high white embankment, each rose erection
the sun makes of glaciers here. This is where traveling

stops: Waste of iced barrow. Fortress of bone. Naked
Eden. Here, nature's choices have narrowed to death,
to survival of those too fit to be kind.
This is necessary, how we lie. When that Lord High Breath

came to Eve, demanding the source of the seed
on her thigh, He knew, of course, already.
For her, then, choice was not at all some rash, heady
option. Not till *after* the eating. Indeed,

it's the same for Clark, Superman, me. Fruit, fig leaf, fakery,
coming home to a hard day's Gethsemane.

THE JOR-EL TAPES

Transcripts of Binary Transmissions Recorded
by the Very Large Array (Socorro, NM)
—Originating in the Vicinity of
Supernova 1993J

Superman is a good cry; and a good cry is half the battle.

—GEORGE BERNARD SHAW
Man and Superman, 1903

THE END OF DAYS

The end of your world will give you pause.
Not the tectonic euphoria
you might imagine: Streets suddenly filled
with a distaste for the horizontal.
Local shopkeepers, the odd dog, abrupt
and incandescent, breaking impossible laws.

Gravity comes to mind, occasional
looting. But not these either. Corpses,
their dusty bouquet. All, of course, miseries
I do not suggest you forget. But then
we are not engaged in exorcising
neighborhoods only, coastal metropoli,

myriad federal (if not eternal)
deficits; these, too, will go to whatever
ground is left more than a bit shaken.
No, the thing about a planet gone to gap
entirely, in *toto*—no stab
at reprieve—is that you still expect

so little from your salvation. A burial
spoon, an onyx spear, a monograph
on galvanic law. A pair of shoes.
Any of these, the knowledge of their having been
left behind, would prepare you for your own
absence, the kind you are used to. You could live,

in other words, with the promise.

KRYPTON NIGHTS

If I could leave my shadow only
behind, the air my body displaced
these many years, the suggestion
of water, night sweat, where just, say,
a cheekbone was before . . . Dread. Even
that I would bequeath you if I could.

Yet, if you've received this, remember
tall sticks planted in the ground at noon.
No, remember there is no this. No
me. No reader, no last planetary
observer. No journal, no witness,
no conclave, no revival, no grand

revolution, no susurration,
no sea to come from, no sun to return
to, no Krypton days, no Krypton nights.
Only charmed figments of electric
residue. This ghost of light, pulse,
silence. Binary diaspora. This me

who I am not but will be soon, if only
briefly, until you turn toward your own
pale sun, the focus shifts, the quality
of light changes, and the shadow you
yourself cast grows shorter or longer
and you find that you've found another

me, and through me, another fragment
of who I may suggest, and soon have
constructed a vast history of, well, your own.
Still, for a civilization of one,
its anatomy is just as real as you
were when I touched you, entered, reemerged.

This, then, is the power of knowing, this death.
When the last Krypton night simmers over
the rim of your world, when we meet in the sky
to find ourselves sharing stars, when what was
once familiar slinks away, disoriented,
hungry for the next clarity, remember

shadows cast from nothing in the dark.

ON JEPHTHAH

On my planet we read books. Our own.
Others'. Little, it is said, escapes
us. Your people have a story,
of Jephthah, the Gileadite. You claim
him unwilling conscience to the carnage
in his blood, his people's. Now what this meant
to your Hebrews—this sacrificial pact
a man made with an often arbitrary
God, the promising up of first meat,
of the first active soul across his
threshold to deitary hunger (this,
the deepest cut your story gives),
the accidental indenture of his only
daughter—what this meant, in exchange for luck
in battle, I have only the vaguest clue.

But from where I stand, from this rock
soon to be but little more than just
that, I can only console one father's
agony with my own. This world, Krypton,
is our child. We, each, may claim the flesh
of each, those pudgy portmanteaus
of skin, cloth, bone, our progeny . . . Yes.
But then, the upshot of all this sex—
the waves we make, riding out the last
few evenings only indescribably
close to being alone, even all those
years of more (at least apparently)
significant evenings, meetings,

falling silk and fallen forms writing
to indistinguish self from seed—all
of this is nothing I can tell you of.

What we have made, we have not made
permanent enough. It is not the child,
not that child's child, not me or the son
I have sacrificed so long before
the others, not my wife, nor her mother,
not her father's long parables
involving light and moving bodies—
it is not the simple loss of all this
which I share with your Gileadite,
but rather that of our true child, the only
begotten fragment of a fragmentary
sun. This *world* is what I offer
to the stars. *It* came, as it came to all
of us here, first. Moving out, breaching
my mother, her lap, that dark and bloody

threshold, *it* greeted *me*. Krypton crossed
then, equally from my perspective,
over into *my* dooryard. And now—
child or no, tambourine or no, menorah
or nothing but a fading yellow star—
we, these people of whom I am one
and whom I, in my decline, choose
to re-adopt through Jephthah, we, I . . .
Oh, my planetary daughter, we may
not understand this calamity you
have brought for us to witness, yet
we recognize the hand by which one points,
one claims, seizing the right to perish
in your name.

THE ELSE

I can only imagine you from your attempts
at God, your artful mediation. From the swell
of that little mustachioed man (those first wartime
broadcasts full of hoops and ladders) to the greenswards
of your word wardens (the *else* they add to each rose
patterned web woven between worlds, the clapboards

of your inadequacies)—from then till now I have heard,
read, translated till my eyes are blue. I know you,
your languages, the irreconcilable
vacuum you imagine between what you say
and what you mean. Not that sublime absence out here,
between what you know and what you imagine I must

imagine, having, unlike you (at least till now) corresponded
with clusters, the sisters, a small turquoise planet
in the system you call Vega. No, this is what we were
made for, it turns out, this joining. Think of your own
roots, the slow ages of ozone, oxygen
and carbon learning to share a common bond.

Single cells wanting company, hot to trot
(you might once have said). For what? The agony,
really, of sharing. Across that data landscape,
from the first primordial actions of those prime
independent agents, from excitation
to inhibition, from pre-condition to Postman,

from worm to Wall Street to the Winnebagos
you've set adrift among the stars, you can trace the pattern,
the long way back to some sub-Saharan mountain. And if
you *have* begun to see us, this connection we've made,
as the same sort of least resistance, as the network
as it might have been, you might also have glimpsed the brain

we were meant to pick, the vast challenge of galactic
consciousness, infinite confusion. But then all this
is moot, nothing more than a hardening
of the arteries, a misremembering, glitch,
a brush with lips whose sordid braille you missed the chance
to read. Knowing (as you will) that there is no more,

that this sector must at last grow mute, that its promise
will speak now only to the unfinished, will you still want
me to have come at all? Or will you, wishing to have looked
elsewhere when searching, make just enough mistakes
to find me, to smell again the smell of your first rain,
supposing that nothing which happens subsides?

JHVH

Is this my world, or yours? It is hard,
with so much information, to keep track
these days of just whose flesh is whose.
I read about an upstart, a ten-year-old,
in your papers. *Summa cum laude,* Bachelor
of Arts. He said, "Finally," as he crossed the stage.

And then there was that plane somewhere over
the Caucasus. No hydraulic fluid.
So they emptied jugs of lemonade
into the lines. When they landed, the pilot,
an atheist, crossed himself and took off
his left shoe. Of that corpse that caught fire

in bed, in its coffin (in Ohio,
maybe Athens), authorities said, "We blame
the embalmer. Or the weather." Your Pope
has named genetic engineering sin.
Yet doesn't even Host begin as wheat,
human intervention? Such are the mysteries

of your age . . . A man born without shoulders
offers to brave a well, reclaim another's child.
A faceless figure in China stands down
a tank. A woman in New York, riding
an escalator, falls through. It grinds her
under heels of those who stare, untrampled.

In Tunguska, some decades ago, some *Thing*
exploded. The trees splayed out like sticks.
It left no crater. When poisoning rocked
the rule of Louis XIV, more than three
hundred nobles were tried for sorcery,
for soaking each other's shirts in arsenic.

Banning fortune-tellers, putting a lid
on the sale of poison, Louis declared
witchcraft a superstition, denied
the existence of any trial, failed
to finesse the record. You look for reason
in the strangest places. For God. For proofs

against. You accumulate accidents,
incidental information, a piece
of rose china here, a political
theory there. You connect, create, slather
layer on layer, ignoring the strain
of the weight of it all and, *some*body's god

willing, escape before the structure sees
collapse. It is easy to dismantle
prevailing sentiments. Easier though
to find joy, at last, confronting the sublime,
to suspect, when disruption knocks,
an ampleness, opportunity.

Some time from now, in the early morning,
perhaps a late, lazy, autumn afternoon,
your astronomers will record the first sign
of non-human, off-world intelligence.
A message. Perhaps this.
I can only imagine.

THE MYSTERIES OF AZAZEL

What if I told you your gods were dead,
and where to find the bodies?
Named some Vatican vault, a tomb in Siam,
a rock-throated grotto
in Venezuela so deep you can see stars
at day? Told you the tale
the Anasazi tell of their leaving?
Explained Roanoke,

North Carolina, its vanished colony, the sign
that read CROATOAN?
Untangled the tasty fate of Earhart? Egypt's
thirty-second dynasty?
DNA perhaps? The alphabet of the Grail,
the asymptotic parameters
of the Rosy Cross? How long before π
becomes regular? When earthquakes?

Why whalesong? Leaf-cutter ants—what's their grammar,
their recipe for kohlrabi
stew? Maybe Buddha? His bones? The first novel
of Lao Tzu? Where *this* Quetzalcoatl,
that raft of snakes, this Ark, the next quark
pair? I could talk to you
about Schrödinger, calm your insecurity
about his cat. Tell you why angels.

Why not mind mites or temporal restrictions.
We have studied you, you

know. Know more than maybe you do yourselves.
I say *maybe*. Perhaps.
It is this word that makes me curious.
Do you understand more
by not knowing? Would you believe that if
you dug half an inch down,

just under the first, crisp, re-entry layer
of the Ka'ba stone's skin,
there you'd find a titanium screw?
Titanium no one's seen
before, unlikely, full of promise? How
about Flight 19,
those fighter planes of yours, or the herb
sequence to animate

a golem? I could tell you anything.
I am alien. First
contact. There are advantages to speaking
first . . . across time. I am dead
after all. Yet my eyes have been others.
When I knew our doom,
I began sharing yours. I have lived this
way, with your lives. I've seen priests,

Punjabi, parochial teachers, the odd sparrow
fall. So, the way to the river
Lethe then? The golden city of Ubar? No, like Troy,
that one's done for. Then how
about the dark night of the soul, its quantum
mechanical effect?
Or the name of the man on the grassy knoll?
His present occupation?

Or what if I gave you a graven stone?
Just that, for all this absence.

THE CURSE OF THE PHARAOHS

My son will be your Moses. He came from a red sea.
Crossing the dark channel between folds between worlds,
he will arrive through the open maw of that jewel-toothed gulf
articulate, astute, uncanny for his age, able
to leap tall buildings in a single bound. It is this last,

though, which will eventually, troublingly, bind him.
What limits can one legislate for him, who is his own
(and only) legislation? Thus, he will have to keep close
counsel. Talk to himself even. Try to speak to the burning
alone, from some high precipice. They are always high.

And, unimprisoned by you, freed on account of the madness
in your hearts, for the purpose of breaking the laws you need him to
maintain, he will, like some gusty god-king, have power over you,
and he will bruise your heel. And there will be enmity
between what he stands for and what he accomplishes

in your midst. And, more than likely, you won't recognize
this, the synchrony of it, not any more than those harried
Hebrew wanderers noticed—passing under Job's coffin,
the heel of Hercules perhaps, or Venus, or the serpent
Hydra—how, just then, my only son was passing through.

THE SECRET DIARIES
OF LOIS LANE

Nothing less than a bursting shell could penetrate his skin.

—JEROME SIEGEL & JOE SHUSTER
Superman, 1938

MAN OR SUPERMAN

I've often heard that every woman wants
one, a Superman to carry her
away. Some singularly divine fellow,
the kind one only meets in movies, alien
to the ways of your average lout.
Imagine Oz. Thor without the thunder.
But what if he knows too much to begin
with, the color of your underwear perhaps?

Or the secret slouch of your breasts, the hang
dog puckers under makeup under eyes
he can read even the *names* of drinks in?
Or suppose further. He doesn't mind.
Remember, your lover won't grow
crow's feet, those whose murderous caws
you've already been hearing for the past
(what?) two years. And when even these begin

to fade, giving way to the kind of embrace
he will surely pity, will you wonder
what he may have seen growing inside
you? What death he may have burned away,
what left behind? What expectation
he may have infected with his own? Will
you hate him then? Or, like some brave new world's
new Magdalene, will you cast away your old

devils, leave him, rise?

GIVE TO HER YOUR CLOAK ALSO

I understand the necessary lie,
that pasty face he passes off for work,
the interest vested in his paper
tiger. But, frankly, three in a bed
is not what I had planned. Each night
that I slip—calling him, from some stark peak
of passion, Clark—the covers grow more
crowded, the issue, more cumulous.

To which side do I cleave then? On which
thunderous thigh do these nails leave
no trace? Though there are times I enjoy
such naughtiness (the occasional
quick one in Perry's office, a hot kiss
on the fly), I still find it hard
to divide time between what he is
and what he's had to hide to be just

that. Don't get me wrong, Diary, I love
the both of him, but these days, when I send
him out for squeeze cheese and chips, when
he comes back, Midway Mart sack in one
hand, would-be thug in the other, I can't
help wondering . . . Should I prefer this
Superman who saves a world a week,
or he who's learned to live his life

by loaning it his cheek?

ORGASM OVER MT. ARARAT

I don't suppose our stars are crossed
on quite the same axis as others'. His, rather
red—mine, yellow. It's a wonder when we fuck
in flight we don't go nova. But that's just it,
isn't it? Love's not about how well we fit
the other's holes. Nor who's got the balls,
or wears the pants, or claims the panty
fetish. That gender stuff breaks down too handily.

No, no matter how alien he may be,
we both began the same. Furrier perhaps.
Lungless even, when we scaled the face of the deep
and, before that, the space between stars—our matter
identical, our evolution parallel.
We both started, for example, with vaginas.
So all that star stuff, what I call the horrible
scope, is no more helpful than religion.

Look at David and Bathsheba, David
and Jonathan, Bathsheba and her maid . . .
No one can tell you just *who* you may claim
for eternity. When that young Babylonian
couple arrived at the top of their mountain,
equal and alone, when Utnapishtim turned
to his bride, promising her the Flood
was done, I bet she jumped his bones. This is how

we fly. Bumper to bumper. Backseat to the sky.

HIS MACULATE ERECTION

Making love to Superman comes easy,
Diary, like riding a perpetual bike.
Considering the contents of his genes,
though, that's another game entirely.
Imagine, for example, his super sperm.
Do those tiny, whipping tails ever flag?
Do they remain inside, set up shop, waiting
for my tubes to, miraculously, untie?

If we play at soap and wandering hands,
if he christens me indiscriminately
in the shower, should we try to plug the drain?
I invent the most frightening scenarios.
There, in the dregs of that porcelain dark,
following raveling threads of sewer,
a billion souped-up cells continue to swim,
blind and eternal, toward the light.

And when the water turns again—past
its requisite recycling plant—back
into some home, innocent, silent, two baths
(probably the suburbs), how will that housewife
explain? I can see her face, her frustration,
all the excuses her long-fixed husband will see
as feeble. Some months from now, maybe a year,
familiar tales will be retold, all the old

fables recycled.

THAT MERMAID AGAIN?

Even Atlantis has to have its vamps.
Since he told me about her, that mermaid,
months ago—about Lori Lemaris, the ex
siren unsurfaced from his past—since then
I've begun, writer that I am, to fabricate
her life. When I imagine myself, sans legs,
curling the wide arc of my rippled flank
through breaker, over riptide, under living

arches of coral and down to my secret
home, I allow myself to curse her.
And admire her. And take her voice, returning
what Andersen, one Hans Christian, stripped
away. I understand. I know. See, my lover
can fly. And though I've had my day
on a Concord or two, though I've fended
off more than your average number

of lowlifes, I can only see through walls
as well as lead. And I've never really gotten
to the bottom of any ocean. Should I blame
my love then? Or those like Hans who deny my soul,
maintaining a need to marry first—to attach
my reach to that of some prick—so testosterone,
somehow holy, can earn for me my entrance
into heaven? Success aside, I still get lost

in Atlantis, that fluted tale, knowing I'd trade nothing for the ride.

THE WEDDING PARTY

Speaking of marriage, I hear his mother
wants me to make an honest man of him.
He laughs at this, his parents' quaint Kansasisms.
But what *would* we do, Diary, honeymoon
on the moon, maybe at that fortress of his
up north, make love under a sky gone mad
with color? And just whom would we invite?
The last few Kryptonian citizens

he keeps corked up in a bottle somewhere?
Supergirl? Krypto, that mutt with super
dog breath? Maybe the members of Justice
League, the Legion, his younger, alternate self?
Oh God, and the party-crashers. Swamp Thing,
Solomon Grundy. *Do you think, Honey,*
I'd ask him, *the Black Canary might warble
a tune or two?* Really, this is serious.

We have no friends (at least not typical,
mortal) whom we could dare endanger.
And how should I prepare? Rice, zinnias,
a slug of anti-kryptonite in my shoe?
Like one of those virgins I used to study
in the Gospels, should I trim my lamp,
prepare for the Bridegroom's uncertain coming?
Or is that long dead world's Last Son

impervious to my burning?

NECROPOLIS

This city, for him, is only a fair
weather fantasy. He knows nothing of death
but the anecdotal. His dreams—I know
he has them—speak not to that which drives
the rest of us to build the monuments
we do. When we flew into New Orleans,
for example, Florence, Nazlett El-Sese
in Egypt, when we read of the latter—

how some dig had dug up the final
secret (the Great Pyramid's construction),
found an ancient harbor that licked and lapped
papyrus plant, once, near the paps of the Sphinx,
how Cheops must have shipped quarried stone there,
where slaves muscled its many tons from less
distance than we'd thought before—he shook
his head, disgusted at what he could not see

as anything but wasted life. Canopic
jars too, those many-headed urns jammed
with the body's imperfect jewels, mummies,
the urge for children even, the pagan plates
adopted by Rome and traded up for tombstones . . .
Nothing which touches the afterlife
touches him. I wonder what he'll do then
when I'm gone. Or Jimmy. Lana. Perry. All

Metropolis? How will it be, this haunted glass necropolis?

LEX LUTHOR'S COMPLAINT
Letters From Arkham Asylum

You cannot touch my planet without destroying something precious.

—SUPERMAN
The Dark Knight Returns, 1986

MIDRASH

Should I lift a leaf from Lovecraft, from Poe?
Explain, oh-so-lucidly, just what sort
of mad I'm not? Tell you all the gorgeous
things I've done were done for my father's sake,
that he beat me when I shaved the cat, bolted
it to a plank of balsa wood, and shot it
through with ions till it spoke? My parents
don't exist. Should I mention that too? The I.
R.S., Customs, Social Security,
the Census Bureau—none of them have records
anymore. I was six when I managed it,
and, though secretly astonished, they punished
me then as well. So I guess I should tell you
how I *do* believe in law, in jurisprudence.
Not in spite of what I've done, but *because*.

The tsunami I whipped up from nothing
back in '78; the hordes of armed
fruit bats who rampaged through the better
part of Metropolis for forty days
and nights; the various forms of techno-
voodoo, hypnosis, cryogenic stasis
I have visited upon one Lois
Lane these many years; the stock market
burps, crashes (both bull market and bear);
all the lionizing I have, quite
unintentionally, directed Superman's
way was meant to mean one thing, one only.
My life, all that I have done, the sentence
I'm now serving, is precisely that:
serving. Not myself, but you, the law.

It's Superman who's broken the social
contract. Mr. Hup-Two-Three, Mr. Big
Cheese in Primary Colors Man. Blowhard.
You move at his every beck, come to his
every call, dream in line with whatever
aliens dream, and—too like that biblical
king, Nebuchadnezzar—mistake the myth
for the message. You *are* the great tree,
the statue with feet of crippled, cracked tarmac,
and he, he is the cobbled stone you've thrown
only at yourselves. He cannot stand
for what he must, by definition, break.
So I must break him for you. Be assured,
while I am here, grazing on grass and locust,
scapegoated to this wilderness, unclean,

cast out, my thoughts are ever with you
and never far from he who put me here.
He will destroy you with his false trinity,
those angry colors he wears. And the rainbow
you see, rising up from the devastation
of order you've tried so hard to cultivate,
will only last as long as he needs you
to serve his final longing, his heaven
brought down to earth. Krypton, I've heard,
was barren at the end. Do not mistake
his purpose. Though you may not believe
it now, already he has bruised your heel,
already he goes to prepare a plot
for you, a final potter's field. What the Man
of Steel has stolen from you is not

purely Occidental.

METHUSELAH

I grow old. Like a rabbi long on Torah
and short on immanence, like some Pharisee
too intent on keeping his temple intact,
I *do* grow old in this gothic greystone,
plotting how to line my palms, his casket,
each imagined cloud, with silver. *Superman.*
Can I go a day without that thug's thorny name
rising up from the stones about me? The others
here, the real loons, they fairly worship him.
Some claim they saw his star fall. No matter
that he (well, he and Batguy) put them here.

Once upon a time, crime was simple. A thief
reaped what he did not sow. Now, what with God
awake in the garden, a good capitalist
(one with head enough for three on his shoulders)
can't even heist an apple without crossing
Yahweh on the way to that other tree—of life.
The gates that give on justice have grown crowded,
packed with polyester rats, too many
in far too little space. They eat their young
on the run between Manhattans (added onions),
luncheons, and benefit backgammon games.

Even these, though, I stomached once. I knew
how to grease their whiskers. Superman
is another story. Armani isn't
his style, and women . . . well, he always had
the best already. The kingdoms of the Earth,

bread, a little peace and quiet—these are not
mine to offer. All I know is how I must
have been born too late, too perfect *not* to
foil. Still, plans are ever legion, and as long
as we're a country where Reagan once wept, crept
crepuscular, where Give-Em-Hell-Harry settled

on settling the East with crematorium
shadows; as long as this remains the place
where Washington longed to face the dollar
with himself, his entourage, a column
of fire; as long as the incommensurate
moments still come and go, like the burning
of Yellowstone or Challenger's bright, brief
spark, I know we won't at last succumb
to him, to the chaos his order implies.
Instead, when I am even older yet—my hands
no longer heavy with his restraining

clause—I will show my grandchildren a torn
cape, some singed tights, and watch them shrink, point,
adorn me with aahs. Only then will I suffer
the interest of children. *Come to me,* I might
say, *trace my tracks, my crow cracks, the long ladder
each scar has become. He thought he was eternal,
but he couldn't grow old.*

THE MODEL

—On keeping busy in the madhouse

First, you must collect the unfamiliar
pieces, this dither, toward a central hub.
Do not, though, mistake pretended order
for any eventual imposition
of form: Albatros, Stuka, Fokker.
Gather what remaining supports you
find—those whose barely-molded planes suggest
horizons—along the end of the space
you've cleared away for your endeavor;
it should be readily apparent which
boundaries you will need. Small parts, recall,
do not imply lesser helpings of discontent,
though they may provoke less delicate
profanities. Can you live (you may be
imagining) with the occasional
prop, shock, spring you've left behind? Early on,
one should watch for false fits that merely seem
expedient. You will need every throttle,
each ambiguous strut, to fill the space
you've vacated for a final version.

Maybe it's not even an airplane,
this craft begun from your departure.
Try not to fret over the wing you mistook
for a stand, the stand you may yet take
for simple ornament; at least the choke
will probably turn out right. Remember,
camouflage hides even the most damaging

evidence of shoddy work. Only
in certain stages is a flush juncture
of, say, hull and hindquarter demanded.
Ruptures along the seams will appear
insubstantial in context—figments even—
with, of course, enough glue. Now, though the primer
you have chosen (its mysterious fumes)
may elicit discussions of vanishing,
though the smell of apples, as it builds
up, is evidence of your mounting
success, though you kind of like the heady
sacrifice such bold exposure permits,
you must account for moderation.

Dote on Wonder Woman now and then,
on her generic, see-through bomber, on how,
in her world, the real McCoy—a B-29,
C-130—must ever be thought transparent.
Following stratagems need to trouble
the potential for failure in any image
you itch to construct of martyrdom.
The blueprints provided for your venture
are, after all, not to be taken
for granted. And though color diagrams
may prove falsely accessible by virtue
of their seeming lack of art, please be assured
you *can* do this. Isn't *this* the vague
rationale that instruction, by definition,
proclaims? Even in another tongue,
the directions model you in future
tense, allowing that you will, at last, finish
construction, that you will need such final steps—
an outline—when you arrive there, moving
still, projecting, on to your completion.

THE DARK KNIGHT OF THE SOUL

is awake as I'm awake, here in Gotham.
Darkly dressed, figmentary, he doesn't bind
against my brain the way Superman is wont.
No, though Batman too skulks the streets, fighting
crime with crime, at least bats make no bones
about hypocrisy. There is acknowledgment
in his very hood—that velvet job with ears
that could be horns, horns that could be emblems
of the devil he denounces even as he serves.

The thing about bats is their adaptation—
each hand grown large, fingers extended, curved
into brittle ribs. And then, the way they've learned
at last to see inside the caul that calls them
out to feed—sonar. Dark shapes bounced back
for capture in those creepy, crass containers
balanced at the axis of each skull. These ears,
it appears, tack them to our terror
spots, invest them with the vestments of night.

They eat mosquitoes, rid us of parasites,
help cleanse our evenings of plague. For just
such gifts, we fear them. What makes one handy,
then, of use in this world, can also make one
horrible. And this, I argue, this—on nights
when I cannot sleep for the sound of two kinds
of flight alight in the heart of our city's sole
darkness—this is how it *should* be.

INSCRIPTION FOR AN ASYLUM

What lack, the perimeter of our knowing, what taste, the purchase of that lapse,
what guile, our denial of absence owing to minds that muster might from each perhaps.

—DR. AMADEUS ARKHAM, 1921

The loons who run the halls here—ever ravished
by a moon that makes odd promises to wed them—
they come to me, and pray, and they are lavished
with my own hysteric offerings of bedlam.

This house was meant to loom a little larger
than the others down these streets of stucco crypts.
But *all* my neighbors—lunatic to barber—
accept this stuffy Superman, his rise and his eclipse,

as if he weren't the golden calf he is.
If *Moses* couldn't brave the face of Jealousy,
who are we to lend a God our eyes?
If all we ever see are but the buttocks of eternity,

if, when the law is handed down, *all* tablets
must break, if what some Hubble sees is a mistake
of taking, too patently, the blueprints
for a universe we'd rather frame than fake,

if even part of this is true and yet you let
proclaimed perfection in a red cape rule you,
something (sanity) there is that you forget:
Rest at the cost of another's rod can fool you.

Thus, the plaque that meets your eye upon the brace
beside this door—the motto that's inscribed here,
Doctor Arkham's only warning—should face
the faces yet within. If entering, beware.

SOME JOKES

I.

Two guys standing on a roof in Metropolis.
One says to the other, "I bet I can leap this
rail in a single bound . . . not get hurt. Wind'll blow
me back like a boomerang." The second fellow,
not to be outdone, takes him up on the wager,
pulls out a sawbuck, lays it on the rail, says, "Sure."

So the first guy straightens his tie, fingers the fall
breeze—an old salt testing his sea—and does a cannonball
over the ledge. Minutes later, winded, he comes back
just long enough to snag his stakes. Two other saps,
watching slack-jawed from across that great, gaping lack
between buildings, see this. Says one to his friend, "Fuck!

Is that guy lucky or what?" His companion passes
it off with a shrug: "That's just Superman in glasses
and a bad suit. How did you *think* he made a living?
Cracking hard cases, occasional skulls, rescuing
every kid, cat, careering train that runs away?"
You know, folks, I ask myself this same thing, every day.

II.

Peter at the pearly gates, shifting from wing tip
to wing tip. When, out for a stroll, Jesus passes, quips,
"Tough job," his favorite ex-apostle (only human),
he who's needed a bathroom break for a millennium,

asks his Rabbi to stand in for a spell. Jesus,
welcoming a new perspective on all this bliss,

says sure. So Peter shows him what to do. "Just
ask a few questions, cross-reference their answers the best
you can with the concordance here. Make certain you stamp
their hands." Some little while later, an old man walks up.
Jesus asks him his name. "In your language? Joseph."
Occupation in the last life? "Carpenter." A brief

recognition begins to cross Christ's mind. He asks him
if he had any children down below. "One. A shame
he wasn't born normally—he came from a star."
Jesus, really suspicious now, asks, "Did he differ
that much from other boys?" The old man nods.
"He wasn't always human, had a voice like God's

that followed him, guided his ways." Jesus, almost
agog now, says, "You loved him." The geriatric ghost
smiles: "He came to me in answer to my prayers."
Elated, Christ asks, "Did he have any marks, scars?"
"Well," the elder offers, "he had nails in his hands . . ."
"Father!" exclaims Jesus. "Pinocchio!" cries the man.

III.

Okay, let's see if I can clear this up. The joke's
on us. We think what we want is Law, primal spokes
on a wheel of cosmic order. What we forget is how
wheels turn, evolve, shift as we shift, restless now
in our rumble seats. We neglect, in the rush to solve
our rat problem, the potential mongoose breeding curve.

Do we really want a savior who will know *every* fall,
hear *each* sparrow's plumeless plummet? This rare bull
we've loosed amongst what only *seems* perpetual—
amongst an inventory of arbitrary rules fragile
as china—is not the Mithra we think he is. We mistake
corrective power for correction. He's no fake

(would that it were that simple), but neither is he Christ
or the Lady in the Lake. The Word made flesh? Worst
case scenario. The Law itself? He can't evolve.
No, the paradigms we build, we build to solve
human equations. Stasis, what his steel jaw suggests,
is only as eternal as our last, best jests.

THROUGH A GLASS, DARKLY

For the letter of the law killeth, but the spirit giveth life.
—II CORINTHIANS 3:6

It was a lovely paperweight, that Bible
Mother used to read me my own mythology
from. She called it a heritage of truth,
named it namable, translatable, steady
as the morning star, saw its message
in the present tense, unwavering, apt.

Though she learned these readings from a suit
some pulpit had ordained, though his ordination
was itself an act of faith, for her, words meant
something we could apprehend. They did not
change, call for interpretation. *For now
we see through a glass, darkly* was clear to her.

Me, I want to know what *for now* suggests.
Is it *thus* now, or *just* for now, now *only?*
And while we're at it, who the hell is *we?*
Paul and his cohorts? The *in* Christians?
Perhaps the Corinthians he's addressing.
But the Jews too? Everyone? Or only

the saved? Then there's this wily little verb, *see.*
See has a long and lustrous tradition
of obfuscation. The first definition:
a seat, a throne, the rank symbolized
by all such butt-rests of authority; the chair
of a bishop, the Church itself, a cathedral

or office of the Pope. Second meaning:
a glance. Third, from the Old English *seon,*
Old Frisian *sia,* Old Norse *séa:* to perceive
with the eye an external object, to become
aware of (in the mind's eye) as in a dream
or vision; perhaps to distinguish

by sight *from* some similar object, to attain
comprehension of, understand, foresee;
to forecast, have a particular mental view
of, appreciate or recognize or believe;
to accept, contemplate, examine, visit;
to know, to be a willing witness, watch

over, take care of, ensure through supervision;
to judge. Which, I ask, will it be? There are more,
to be sure—several shaky columns
in the trusty O.E.D.—but then we must
remember, these are *English* variants,
not the original Greek. What might

Longinus have seen in the word, that scholar
of the sublime? Moving on, it gets even
trickier. *Through.* Is this to be taken
in the instrumental sense? By means of?
Or shall we infer the local, more simple
sense: *through* a glass? Preposition, nothing

more. What then of this *glass* itself? Are we
talking a window here? I understand
their panes were made of mica back then.
Hard, I imagine, to see through. So vision,
Paul says, is inherently impaired—the world
outside, a grainy, imperfect substitute

for the real, the ineffable probably
already before us. Something we can't,
with mortal discretion, judge. But this assumes
too much. *Glass,* for the Elizabethans
(this version comes, after all, from the days
when Shakespeare had not yet bequeathed his wife

their second-best bed), *glass,* for King James' crowd,
did not have to be transparent. The word,
for them, meant also and more properly
a mirror. So we see *as through a mirror.*
Wait a minute. Let's be confused *together*
for a while. How does one see *through* such

a thing? One doesn't. One sees what is behind,
the hinder portions of God, perhaps, the back
water regions of ourselves, our history,
the shadow in the corner of some Corinthian
hut, what we never were, what the world
might be if we could spin on one heel

fast enough. But, as always, by the time
we turn, it's gone. Whatever *it* was. Then is
this just another version, a prefiguring
if you will, of that famous Alice, of her own
linguistic confusion? She, too, had to play
hide-and-seek with a mantel full of babble.

Finally, then, we come to *darkly.*
Mirrors, the most ancient ones, were imperfectly
polished metal, the reflections they managed,
obscure. *Darkly* may suggest this. Paul
may mean that what we see, we see obscurely,
as if *through* mica or *in* a mirror.

But might not he also be speaking
to that which we perceive, *always,* darkly,
glass or no? The glass, then, not *glass* but flesh?
Our eyes themselves? The perception we adopt
of seeing? I could linger on the modern
schematics of how eyes really work—the world

coming to us, as it does, upside down—
how image is only that, an image,
and discuss the implications (what even
Goethe troubled himself over) of light,
because, well . . . See, things have no color,
only properties of absorption, reflection,

and . . . But perhaps more to the point, *darkly,*
literally and in the Koine dialect,
is not *darkly* at all. James' boys took
certain liberties. The Pauline version
reads ἐν αἰνίγματι, for the layman,
in an enigma. We could read this, then,

adverbially, as in: *for now we see
through a glass, enigmatically.* But back
when we were still stealing enough ambiguity
to make our language interesting, *darkly*
probably worked better, had more charm,
less clarity, more, well, enigma

in and of itself. God, in the Septuagint,
uses the same word referring to Moses:
"With him will I speak mouth to mouth, even
apparently, and not in *dark sayings.*"
Here, the enigma is still dark—our translators
preferring poetry to what we might

call pure—but the question is, can the Word
be pure? Should it? New Covenant or Old,
King James, Living, Revised, New English,
Jerusalem? The versions of versions revised
through each dark seeing, translated through eyes
and on to brains where hearts, more than hands,

take over . . . Well, isn't the point of Christ's
coming a return of power to each of us,
each woman and man who might not even have
seen the temple curtain tearing? Incarnation
validates the holiness of perspective, each
vessel, each glass, this limited, lush

glory of confusion. This is what we are.
Not supermen, not perfection dressed
in our garish, red, blue, and yellow Sunday
best. We, the world we read, are Torah.
Superman, the constancy of his concupiscent star,
is less than this. A big red *S.* A text

we read too lightly.

BOOK TWO
AMAZON DAYS

*You may break your chains. But you must wear these
wrist bands always to teach you the folly of
submitting to men's domination!*

—APHRODITE
Wonder Woman #1, 1942

*And I have known the arms already, known them all—
Arms that are braceleted and white and bare . . .*

—T. S. ELIOT
"The Love Song of J. Alfred Prufrock," 1915

I, WONDER

Question is, would I matter if I didn't
tout these tits? If my legs weren't, total,
seventy-two inches of eye candy?
And get a load of the get up . . . Well, if
it doesn't get you up, you're more than
mostly dead. Whitman said *there is that lot
of me and all so luscious,* but then he
didn't have to hide the *lot* in a hanky.

Try fighting Hirohito in heels, Nazis
in a nightie, crazed crackheads with the wind
wolf-whistling up your crack. I defy
you guys to name just one super savior,
one with a prick, who lets it all hang out.
Sure, they leap about in longhandles, uber
Underoos, but even Underdog unzips
more than me before hiking a leg.

So, okay, definitely not a dog.
It could be worse. I could look like Lois,
maybe Hawkgirl after a turkey shoot.
But when I hear that other busty bombshell say
I'm not bad, I'm just drawn that way, I have
to wonder, do alien androids really need
to know I have nipples? Does Wonder Man
buy Nair by the crate? Shanna the She-Devil,

does she worry over her pits? I don't
suppose I've ever had another option.

It's all about cleavage, and I don't just mean
what I could do with an arrow and a dozen
ax heads. To do what I do—saving you,
in this world that would, otherwise, have me
Amazon, Amazon only—to do it dirty,
hairy, in a jumper, to do it plumper

would beg the old joke. You know, the one
about that kid. Let's say Tim. To save himself,
his town, and the like, he had to stick his finger
in the dyke. She beat the shit out of him.

OUR BODIES, OURSELVES

An Echo by W. W.

It's funny how one girl can be two people.

—WONDER WOMAN
WONDER WOMAN #4, 1943

PRINCE

If Mother could only see me now . . . as a very feminine woman . . . a nurse no less, in a world full of men.

—PRINCESS DIANA
Sensation Comics #1, 1942

I. UTOPIA

We all leave Paradise. I left my prints
there, on everything, when I was young.
Each orchid, every smooth grove of olive, tongue
of Turk's cap, on silverswords, archer fish, hyacinths,

on even the tarsiers and turtles, as if my hands
had to know the shapes of all I would soon be
letting go. The trade I made was no Thermopylae,
no Miletus, but my mother's promise, these bands

I wear, bound me to more than just my sisters,
their island, their Amazon days, my own lonely nights.
So when, near the end of Paradise, down by its bights,
that man washed ashore, a man as lost to the bluster

of disaster as we had once been; when, still waterlogged with war
he saw me, said, *Woman* . . . Why wonder that I brought him to my
    door?

II. ESSAY ON MAN

He saw me, said woman, as wonder, what brought
him to my door. Both urge and end, his own long fall.
But I was no soldier, not then. The din and drawl
of war remained as abstract as his fever-fraught

dreams. Oh, and what fine fancy I must have starred
in! Though I spent days tending my flyboy's wounds,
though he understood, intimately, the sound
of my voice, the fact of my hand as it carried

his own to my breast before he died, even then,
with memories of his mission, his crash, returning,
with all the inconvenient evidence of my being
real, still he wanted me as Valkyrie, as sin.

Me, from a land where he was just in jest.
He, from a land where I could only arrest.

III. COMMON SENSE

He, from a land where I would only arrest,
where kiss and fist were lovers that caressed,
where men were women's last excuse for less.
History-, mystery-, breast-, vagina-less.

It's a wonder we could communicate at all.
Even when I brought him back, used our science—a small
matter, but as far from his own as cathode from caul—
even after I'd dragged him back from death's mead hall,

even then, he imagined me imagined manna,
saw me as a proof of God, perhaps Valhalla.
But then I guess *he* . . . He was what? Shangri-La
to me? Abomination? Something new. Our law

said he could not stay, but also not to kill.
They'd need a hero to bring him back. They need one still.

IV. VINDICATION OF THE RIGHTS OF WOMAN

They needed a heroine to bring him back. Need?
One still wonders if indeed they needed *me*.
Then. The distance from that world to this, agreed,
was not so fraught with fright as mine to his, but he

was still with me then. I counted myself
lucky to have a steady job. Though keeping him
out of trouble left me breathless, it's not as if
there was a dearth of dastardly to help keep trim.

No, I don't know that—on coming to your shores,
on finally finding a place for the plane, the rest
all which vanishes desires—that the mores
of this land struck me as particularly less,

or how you herded unheard women was, well, surprise.
All I knew was what I gained, a ewe lost in eyes.

V. THE RIGHTS OF MAN

All I knew was what I gained, a ewe lost in eyes.
Here, they were ubiquitous: catcalls, gawks, cocks,
assward assumptions. After one has fought for the prize,
beaten better sisters to blood and sand, one balks

when, even *after* the arena, the audience remains.
Back in Paradise, I had to earn the *right* to be banished,
had to win the Games, master chains, take the reins
of my kanga mount and—so tasked, masked, I vanished—

prove myself to my mother, placate the Queen,
salve the substance of my dream. Saving even one man?
It seemed, in the end, such a small endeavor,
returning him to what he was: Capt. Steve Trevor.

But leaving didn't relieve me my star status. It stuck,
the liberty of the lamb. I never learned to pass the buck.

VI. THE SECOND SEX

Libertine or lamb, I never learned to pass the buck.
But *had* I passed him; had I left him to another,
to my sisters to save, let him die, invited a quick fuck
and even quicker forgetting; had I made him brother,

friend, astonishing but temporary, acquaintance
only; had I left this world of yours to its own
devices, all that power piled up (no maintenance)
between your legs; had I eschewed the throne

of this Regent, that Reich; had I abhorred your war
altogether, left you, left him, to fend for yourselves;
had I abandoned you all to sea, to mountain, at my door,
all I ever learned from dodging bullets—shells,

lead—would've been to not end dead. Instead, my blunder?
I shared with him my shackles. Is it any wonder?

VII. THE PRINCE

Woman I shared with him. But my shackles?
I wonder. Perhaps that's what I've left on the altar
for all of you. By being this being that's lack-less,
eternal, Hercules strapped in a backless halter,

by sharing my shoulders, my ripples, my pecs,
my faith in the failure of some guy with specs,
by fighting, as praxis, your axis, your evil,
becoming your Eve and survival, your rival,

by leaving my land for apotheosis,
by being both symptom and prognosis,
well . . . Bombshell or no, I've left you ticking.
I've left you what's left after apple picking.

I've left you it all. Pain. Common sense.
What we all must leave. Paradise, I left my prince.

PRINCESS

I wonder if I am getting jealous of my other self.

—DIANA PRINCE
Sensation Comics #3, 1942

I. PHAEDRUS

Princess? My eye. Leaving paradise, we all
want to believe we were *more* before, not less.
Yes, it might be easier not to dress
ourselves in wristlets, gown, the long fall

we once wore in another land, that last life.
Easier to go forward undiminished, believing
ourselves ever larger than we were, but the thing
is, we tend like rats to follow the fife

into the mountain, run up short against the wall,
look back and see what children we were, following
too, and want never to have left. Swallowing
what we've chosen is hard. No, better to call

back to that other self, say, *Don't leave town,*
than admit you're more a princess, now you have no crown.

II. EVERYMAN

To admit I'm more princess now that I've no crown
is to say that what I had was not what I remember,
to believe this life, success dressed as Wonder
Woman, preempts Paradise. W.W., that clown,

bests Prince, Princess? I guess I'm just confused,
tired of being more choice than myself, better than what
I was, more Goddess less the gods. Not fat,
like Etta. Not pawn, dear Steve. But used,

used to win the prince, to trump this very Prince
that I've become. Yet who am I to hate what I've made?
To envy myself the tickertape, accolade, parade?
Still, when I put on those tights, saved Steve from stints

in the stockade, from Poison—oh, the perils I could list—
why was it the lie he loved and not the lonely typist?

III. THE FEMININE MYSTIQUE

Why the lie? Was it love? The lonely
typist? I know Kent ducks such dramas
too, but by Hecate, for him it was *only*
two. Me? I'm a fucking trinity. Mama's

girl. Heroine. Mouse. Why is it us,
women, always, stuck with messier mental houses?
Triplicate Girl? Huntress? Lightning Lass?
Oh, and then if we cross the abyss,

the dark divide between simple detective
and, well, marvel, there's Marvel *Girl,* née
Jean Grey, a.k.a. Phoenix, a.k.a.
Dark Phoenix, later a whole host of prospective

relations, reincarnations. Ever only *almost* one.
It's always "we," $3/\infty$. Virgin, mother, crone.

IV. FROM RITUAL TO ROMANCE

It's always *we*. Three over infinity preside.
Virgin: she before the he is seen inside.
Mother: she because the her is just a ride.
Crone: me, when at last I let the one decide.

Of course I know it's not that simple.
The world turns on more than just a dimple,
the crack in everything. But what of the wimple,
the *chador, burqa?* Aren't they there to hide the ample

firstness of what men can never be? The West—
your madness, not mine—rewrote the best
seller of all time, biology, to make us last.
Problem is, the penis is just a clitoris

with choler. You want us. You want what you've lost.
But everything you do divides the conquered by the cost.

V. ALLEGORY OF THE CAVE

Nothing that you do divides the conquered.
The cost, yes, makes us, me, crazy. I don't want
to be all you suspect, everything you've feared
since you first crawled bawling from the haunt

you call caves, the origin you want to believe
was not your mothers, but then at least a third
of what I am I owe to you. And that cave
me, that cave *of* me, what I name Word,

the beginning, what I dragged even Steve
Trevor to, hauling him from one origin, the sea,
to another, that me, that Paradise, I can't leave.
It can't be covered, broken as I am broken. See,

I guess in being three—me, less than me, and the me who,
in saving you, pulls you all free—I'm only two.

VI. LEVIATHAN

In saving you, pulling you all free—I'm only two.
I *am* the me who left paradise to save it,
but also she who jealously watched her man *covet*
me, tart in tights. So, yes, two. Or one. You

know as well as I the history of the divine,
the need for opposition, enemies, hell,
self or other. Leviathan, Yahweh's handyman.
Seth, Osiris' brother. Inanna and Ereshkigal.

But these are only those who complement,
shadows, the big id tease. Gilgamesh, king of ease.
Enkidu, man of moss. Frigg, woman of omen.
Hel, liaison to loss. Huck and Jim. Thelma, Louise.

None of them are only one. Yet, their troubles, mine.
So much to do, love, save. So many schizos, so little time.

VII. THE DESCENT OF WOMAN

So much for love. I've saved so many—schizos
most of the time—but not myself. Me. One version
of those other doubles doubled over with guilt, bozos
built, like Wonder, on angst and alliteration.

Peter Parker, wimp, poisoned by a spider.
Matt Murdock, blinded by radioactive canister.
Bruce Banner, werewolf, green, wanderer
in the world. Dr. Don, lame, God of thunder.

Susan Storm, Shiera Sanders, Greer Grant,
all broken, fractured, bent. Still, as strong
as Clark Kent. Best and worst of both worlds. *Can't
we all just . . . Okay,* you say, *just get along*

little Princess. But I can't. I left leaving when I left said
Princess, my I, leaving Paradise. We both did.

PARADISE BOUND

By Hippolyte, Queen of the Amazons

For you, O bridegroom, there was never another girl like this one.

—SAPPHO
The Poetry of Sappho, ca 600 B.C.E.

PARADISE ISLAND

I sing of arms and of a woman who fate made
fugitive, who on her arms *wore* arms, bracelets, bonds
I forged myself from folly. First to journey
from the coasts of this, our island paradise, she
became our hope, your truth trope, my only daughter.
Diana, queen of air, princess of water. Her story
still courts the corners of your dreams, endless,
artless, homespun, virgin as her origin.
But though the tale is simple—a girl, an island,
the plane—I know it's one you won't remember,
the girl not your average girl, nor island anything
you'd imagine. Then let us begin with an end,
recover a foundling race, one that never lost
a battle, fought foe they couldn't best one abreast.
God was still Goddess then and women, those you now name
Amazon, ruled the better part of this man's world.
Yet, next to no trace remains. Their nation—full
ration of estrogen, women, women only—
made one mistake. They trusted me, and I, another.

Herakles, that ass, set himself more than martial
tasks, settled on *us* to test his ninth grasp, deceit,
the old story. Once we'd beaten him, he and Ares'
armies, once I'd made him beg, attended him, his wounds,
words, the poetry he bled, let him into our camp,
my bed . . . Afterwards, after orgasm and Ovid,
after *all* the sheets had run red, he rose, stole
the source of our power, the girdle bequeathed me
by Aphrodite and enslaved us all. It was then

I prayed and, angered, Love answered. Yes, she sheared
our shackles, broke chains threaded through the yoke
of our shame, unleashed our strength link by link and let
us wreak revenge on those who would have used us
as they willed. But those shackles themselves, cuffs
that killed, we promised we would always wear. *Swear,*
our Goddess said, so we did and followed her across
waves, over sea, over dead men's graves to this
island, here, where we took an oath of peace, re-made
Greece, made what women must always make alone. Life
without end, forever a-men.

                              Millennia passed, death
like earth-breath rose and fell until one day, turning
from my Magic Sphere, Athena's scrying eye,
one day, under aegis of Hera, Diana, Love
herself, one day, instead of throwing earth to curve
the contours of a pot, I shaped myself another
self, a child, tot unlocked from clay, toddling Goddess.
And she grew, stronger than Herakles, swifter
than Mercury, yet, sadly, no wiser than me.
When the plane came, crashing to our shore, iron
Eagle made meteor by the vagaries of war,
when my one true love found she loved its pilot
above even the land she found herself fallen in,
heavier than he, when she offered to take him back,
see to his needs, do for him, his people, deeds
that would save them all from another of Ares'
plots, I should have seen the me I'd molded into
her, I should have herded him home myself. Instead
we held the Games, the great Contest, to name a heroine.

Banned but still bold, disguised, she won every round,
donned the costume I'd made from a flag I found

in the wreckage. From blood and steel, then, her future.
And that's how she left us, Paradise, Themyscira,
city of her "birth," left us for the best of Earth.
The rest you know. That war was won, at least some
seconds, though whole artilleries of lechery lay
ahead. She became a nurse first, then secretary,
always chained to men who remained in charge. It's as if
she, we, had never learned. Herakles is Herakles,
War war. Sleep with Hephaestus and you get burned.
And yet somehow she managed, conquered the frump,
the glasses, men that matured like blackstrap molasses,
kept herself whole, and *earned* those bands that, more than hands,
showed you what your world could be. See, coming to her
is coming to me, our island, arriving at what it means
to be fettered *and* free. So that Captain came, took
one away. So what?

                    This is how it's always been,
some man leaving with the best piece. Even the myth,
the story you tell yourselves of who and where we are,
that too is part of your forgetting. You want
there to *be* island, woman, a place of respite,
a cave that craves your head, but you want it *away,*
want it lost, only to be remembered when you need,
when, in the long dark, what you've made of yourselves
comes back, cracks up on shore, reminds you of another
possible way. You want it, us, your Wonder
Woman only when—suffering, in pain—you can
recall that way safely, and come to us, and ask
forgiveness. Why else would you know so much
about Bats, that guy in a cape, but not her? Why just
the great *male* escape? In your comics, your modern
myths, there stand three, three who owe more to eternity
than all others combined. Yet you come for my daughter

only when the other two fail, when dark knights
and even brighter tights seem too frail. Oh my captains
of industry, my trembling Trevors . . . Oh you,
my starry-eyed Steves, tell me, what will you do
if *this* Eagle stalls, your last heroine falls, leaves, reaves?

THE GREEN WAY

Imagine perfection. No. Now try again.
Forget everything, every ought you thought you
knew. The names of the mothers, faults of fathers.
    Literature, each

imperfect Oedipal yawp. Art, all that cracked
paint, all the gunshots and opium and ears.
Inventions, from upright spine to speech to rocks
    to, well, anything

Einstein might have said. Forget each failure
it's taken to bring you here, each reach that ends
in grasping, straw. Of course you'll wonder what you
    left, exactly, when

you arrive, what lust for that last life lingers
yet. You will regret so many things. Toasters
and cinnamon and butter and bread. Mornings
    at your grandmother's

house. Sitting on her porch on a swing in front
of a window through which the smell of sweet
potatoes wafts. You will, thinking about that house,
    about its coming

down, regret the summers spent there, remember
attending, say, a sun dance where some Sioux
flute player asked you to close your eyes and place
    yourself in a space

of pure peace. You will remember the surprise
you felt upon closing yourself down only
to open again on that porch, the clutch
        of your gut when, just

this past week you saw its roof roofing only
ground, chimney sunk to the cellar, swing gone,
smells, mere hypothalamic haunting. At first,
        the question, *What do*

I have, will not occur to you. Or, if it
does, you will try to replace anything real
with the fiction of all you think you own, are.
        This is not you. No,

nor even memory, or melancholy,
or regret. The women you have hurt, houses
you've haunted, pale poems, pandemonium,
        all that you've herded

into meaning. From Athena's Magic Sphere
to Phaistos disk to Holy See, Edison's
eidolon, Sagan, side B, Hubble's hobbled
        lens, sins, DVD . . .

From what you remember to what you now see,
symbol, image, empire, empty reverie,
grandmother, girlfriend, vacation, trowel, cape,
        comic, atomic

ship for making your escape . . . None of this is
what you have, what you'll find in, well, coming here.
All you've run away from, all that you hold dear.
        Woman or island,

your land or my land, bit part or A-list,
heroine, typist. Nothing matters. It all
does. When you leave the machine, accept the green
　　　of my forgotten

isle, aisle of the way, the *I'll* of another
day left wanting, know this is how it *should* be.
Loss. Remember the poet who said the *rest*
　　　is dross and let it

go. Go forward into the green, pass on
that pale sheen, the language of book and scholar
dander, tourist gander, neon, freon, sales
　　　hook. Pitch the wounded

world of men, sans which you thought you'd fall, and fall
anyway, for anemone and February
Daphne, silk snake's head, Solomon's seal and sea
　　　poppy, Venus maiden-

hair, fair resurrection fern. Imagine some
woman you've left, some house, some hope you barely
recognize. Okay. *Now,* open your eyes, breathe, and
　　　enter Paradise.

SACRED SITES

So many of them. Take, for instance, this
smooth plain just off the shoulder. You have been
here before, pressing yourself to leave
less inviting paths behind. To linger
at the nape, this crest behind a whorl
of landscape, its darker tresses, would seem
easy, but having yet to offer what
it is you must, you seek invitation
further on. Approaching each slow rise
which heaves to fill as if breath beneath you,
you encounter, finally, a brace of stones
molded like small hogans, pebbled, erect.

Here, you leave the first of many prayers.
Letting your hands tease their surfaces
a moment only, you fumble forward
toward a depression you can just make
out in the vale ahead. Past this, you know, lies
another grotto, deeper, cut into
a swelling your eyes alone have followed
far too long. Tangles, briar-like, smelling
of musk, mist, sweetgrass close about you,
distractions as necessary as the wet
you find beading gooseflesh to a boil.
This has been a harder journey than you
imagined.

         Setting out, all you knew was
that this holy place, this ancient quarry

where blood, the People's blood, has long been
mined, this secret cleft where myth and mind
entangle, this was where you'd hoped to breech
what walls you feared had closed you off from wanting.
Now, hands painted red, supplicant, skin torn,
breast pierced, face streaked, and body given up
to that ground from which it rose, you lie
among clay, *as* clay, created before
creator, and lift up your voice and lift
up your heart, and, holding closed the gapped flaps
of a chest from which you've torn it, you offer
all you have, the dearest passages you know.

THE BREATH OF LIFE

clay \'klā\ n **1:** *plastic earthy material*
used in making pottery which becomes
permanently hardened by firing **2:** *earth,*
ground, mud **3:** *the mortal human body*

      carved from a corpse, all curves and cornices,
      the universe was, for the Babylonians, bound
      by water, by woman, the Tigris and Euphrates.
      The god of light made rivers from her eyes

in Egypt where they understood that Earth crowned
bloody and primeval from between her thighs,
Nut was a warrior. Her glyph, two crossed arrows
set against skin. Later it would mean *weaver*

from the Torah, from the *first* creation, this:
    "And God created man in his image . . .
      male and female he created them." Even
    Elohim. Plural. Curious feminine ending

      after the flood, after they emerged alone
      from their chest, Deucalion and Pyrrha heard
      God's voice. It said, "Throw behind you the bones
      of your Mother." From stones, then, the rest of us

know that in the Gnostic Gospels, God says, "I am
the Womb to the All . . . the glory of the Mother."
Later, "I am the whore, and the holy one.
I am the wife and the virgin . . . the daughter"

Spider Woman, who made the sun from turquoise,
  white shell, red and yellow rock, spun the world
    from a purple glow and us from herself, a bit
      of her own being. Always a few more threads

        to placate Pele—creatrix of sea matrix, island
          garlands, eruption itself, the cone called Mount
            Kilauea—one sacrifices young. Men licked clean
              with her tongue, tossed back as black blood, healing

a great clay griddle balanced on mountains.
This, they say in Columbia, is what Romi Kumu
made. The sky. The Earth she shot forth in fire
from her seething sex. Her orgasm, us

another, an Aztec, also made the ground
  quake. Coatlicue fashioned the world, this primal
    bauble, from her lava altar. From Aztlan,
      her seat on that high peak, she sets us swaying

        holding the multiverse in her womb, her breasts—
          the moon and sun, two parts only of that all
            encompassing passion (procreation, the thousand-
              petaled lotus)—are Devi-Shakti's great gift

claiming he too could make life, a man once
tried to shame our mother, Mawu. Carving
a person from a banyan tree, he breathed on it.
When nothing happened, she planted him with death

what some scientists believe our mother to be
  is indeed dirt, the latter our ladder, the true
    rag and bone shop where the heart starts. Clay.
      Electrochemically alive, asleep and waiting

my touch. It awakened her, my daughter, my budding
godling. How? All I know is the making
of my dearest dreidel, my gorgeous little golem,
took hands, a woman's hands and clay, clay

to carve each leg, each coltish curve, the unopened
petals of her sex, her power, her charms, ribs,
arms, the strong line along a jaw. I ran my hands
over her, smoothing, worshipping what began

raw only to become supple, fair, then, everywhere,
skin. Skin the color of menses, the color of pain
and patience and pity. This is how one shapes
the world. Abstractions, Goddess, the moon's dark blood.

Until she breathed, the whole world held its breath.

GOD'S CLITORIS

In the sixth day of Her blood moon, God came
to the woman, lonely, whispering words
of longing. The woman, naked and new,
freshly pressed from the loins of a power
now returned to her, submitted, turning
to the light that settled itself beside her,
took on form (clavicle, lip, vulva, breast), cast
back the shadow from her eyes, and let herself see
Her. All evening and morning that seventh day

they lay together in the long grass, God's tongue
snaking its sudden way into female flesh,
parting the other's already opening folds
the way Her breath might ply a path in some
saltier sea. The woman held on for life,
her own tongue sliding deep into mystery,
lips locking down on the divine. Splayed
this way, wet and alive with the hasty taste
of one another, fingers lingering between

legs, straying between clefts, nipple biting
nipple, bending back a moment only
then snapping past to lose itself in the lush
growth just beyond, arms thrown back to grapple
with what neither could fully grasp, the earth
itself began to turn. The woman, nameless,
breathless now, and buried between her maker's
thighs, thrust first one knuckle, then another
into the unplumbed deep bent on swallowing her,

pitched her own weight—deep against deep—against
that face she had ridden up from nothing
to this garden on, and came. God stroked her
from beneath, beyond, knowing this was the one
the universe, She, had chosen to shuffle
off Her substance for. Knowing, too, why and how
soon, too soon, She would be forced to lose her
to another. This one pulled fresh and steaming
from the woman's side. Her blood, his blood.

THE BERMUDA DEPTHS

I have never not been frightened by the deep,
nor not attracted, too, by that below
which must, since it's its nature, cast off sleep,
surface, promise knowledge of the slow
oppressive ages that accumulate
like regolith, barnacles on backs
of beasts that know no light.

               The primate,
it is said, was once in love. Perhaps
it missed what waves we once refused our hearts,
or maybe something lacking in the trees
suggested leaving. Regardless, the shards
of who we'd not become, some rogue species
of discontent, knuckled us back to brine
where dark, uncanny swells we'd never stop
returning to suckled us naked.

               That high shine
the sea assailed us with then, this macabre
nudity . . . Well, likely it's exposure
finally we fear, that or the unforeseen
pull of what wooed us once already from the pure:
banyan, branch, the unsullied lurch each green
monkey feels about her gut the moment
she leaps.

          I myself am indifferent anxious.
Here—trapped between one vast, lost continent

and the next, adrift among what spaces
must result—islands, I've discovered,
aren't enough, the little love they offer,
but a shadow of respite. Unrecovered
from that doom the womb teaches, we suffer
our days dog paddling down the Aegean,
crossing, glossing deep upon deep, first same as tenth,
our least desire become Fijian
mermaid, false, or, worse, coelacanth
only believed extinct.

        Still, I too have heard myths
of those who've made it to their rest undrowned,
reaching at last the tortoise back. *There's no abyss,*
they say. *It's turtles all the way down.*

THE ABYSS

Every month, it is woman's fate to face the abyss of time and being, the abyss which is herself.

—CAMILLE PAGLIA, 1990

The depth at first is something that must start-
le even one who knows the price of such end-
eavors. The sheer drop says nothing should all-
ow return, let alone a safe descent, but none-
theless, we understand that *none* of this is us-
ual, real even. The need to fall, the them-
atic significance of expulsion and return, the *au-
thor's* need that is always also the heroine's, dispar-
ate plot points which call for a kind of pres-
cience, a turn perhaps at Paul's pretend pul-
pit . . . All of this is specious summary, curs-
ory overview. The myth of the heroine's grac-
ious consent to fall *for* us, to become some hol-
istic statistic for the race, to enter unlikeness, part-
icipate in laughter, disaster, slaughter, bawdi-
ness, love of the chaste? Sophistry. Not sol-
ution. The heroine *is* because she is more than empti-
ness, abyss, unleaped lack, an unfinished line ful-
filled only after. It's not even precisely her, an id-
ea that *isn't* yet, but rather the *potential* for, the art-
ifice.

THE DEATH OF THE AUTHOR

By William Moulton Marston, a.k.a. Charles Moulton,
inventor of the lie detector, of DISC theory,
of Wonder Woman

And all went still, as if the eternal moved transverse across the mortal.

—SHARON OLDS
"S," 2002

THE SEDUCTION OF THE INNOCENT

Forget Lucifer,
forget Luthor, call *me*
Lord of Lies. William
Moulton Marston, psycho-
logist, feminist,
cartoonist, poetaster,
Zoroaster, master
of the heart's Descartes:
I wink, therefore I am.

Wonder was always
mine. Before I made *her*—
she of the XX oasis,
eagled ecstasis,
Aphrodite nightie—
before my princess
of Paradise premiered,
I learned the arteries'
artifice, sin's systolic

shhhh, the hush of blush,
luster of bluster. Nothing
could escape my snare.
Not one woman. Not
two. Not the one I
made of my wives,
gave a lasso to, bound
with that other
invention, my intention

to save us all from men
like me. My deity,
detector of tricks, love's
protectrix, distaff
of polygraph, Diana . . .
From her, from you,
I learned every lie,
how the heart is awed
by fraud thy god, by tonic

of the comic, dissembling,
the power of trembling,
all the universal
monsters. Once, these too
were mine. When
Hollywood knocked, I talked,
taught magic to the lanterns
there. Call me lector,
doctor of sign's design.

Even Frankenstein
believed truth comes dead,
heart or head, and love is all
we have to set it
stumbling. I submit
I know what you desire,
understand fire, more than you
yourself suspect of trust.
The Lord? *She* said, "I am lust."

WWW.AMAZON.COM

Alive! he cries, *It's alive!* And the Doctor
has done it. Among Bunsen tungsten and Tesla
vesicles, between vast glass phallus and an opening
like lips in the castle roof, between creator
and created a spark has passed. But it's not
about that moment, is it? The final frames. No,
it's what comes later. Creation, creature, monster,
maid, all follow only *after* the madman dies.

Meaning isn't made under sheets, no, nor
on them, but in the dark spaces where what
we've modeled meanders from hut to hut
looking for a way to make the former pay,
make him form more, more like what's been
formed already. And so the maker is made,
the made made maker. What we wanted,
well . . . The search, for Whale, was not far off.

His sequel, even better than the first, rose
on familiar limbs, cast the same canted shadows:
Same town, same castle, same stupid mistakes.
Begin with murder, end with a couple of kites.
Bandages. Breasts. Lightning hair highlights.
The Bride awakens, she sees her mate, then,
as always, a castle crumbles. Fear, caress,
hiss, bloody mess. Later, imitations, a thousand

incarnations. Myself, I made my *own* woman,
made a woman to make *her,* constructed an island

on which they lived and a history, men, to justify
the paradise they'd escaped to. I shaped a man
who shaped *them*. A man cast from the castings
of other men. Hercules, hero turned heavy.
And he? Molded by Mars. So what about me? Wives.
I wanted to understand them, them and men.

But I found women don't need understanding, only
their own place, an infinite space to be made more
of. And so, since the Princess, since Diana—she
who I tooled to school a patriarchal world—since
then, I've watched her from the grave, watched
from the only place an author *can* watch, proud
of the parade, our hottest Goddess, American maid.

I've seen her, her signs, her life lines, evolve. First

Wonder Woman, then Girl, then Tot, Justice
Society, League, the Titans, Super Friends.
I've seen her storm the comics—*Sensation, All
Star, Cavalcade*—breeze in and out of news, loom
large on *Ms.* And down the years I've watched
other watchmen groom her for Goddesshood.
Stripped of power in '68, turned wanderer
in the earth like a candy Cain, a runway

reject, psychedelic go-go booted bra burner.
Then the Seventies. William Woolfolk's ex's hexes,
the attempt to bring her back, maybe, maybe,
then Samuel R. Delany, more powers, black
sister (even TV kissed her, from Crosby to Carter,
that long-missed world, in a single season), plus split-leg
scissors, cocoa cans, cake pans, blow up dolls, cartoons,
tattoos, Underoos, Wonder Bread, Wonder Bra . . .

On and on, through the first uncursed women
writers, artists, married then crisised then dead,
devolved to clay. Then once more re-rigged, rebooted
with so many other mothers, other earths, her eagle
recast as two-tasked, as hieroglyph, *W* nested in *W,*
a sign in love with flight. Then the breaking of chains,
of laws of mammary gravity, at odds with Artemis,
stripped of her mantle, dressed down to sidekick,

resurrected again, killed, again. And, at last, Goddess
of Truth, given flight, made into *her* mother,
mother herself. Both times, Superman. A broken-
backed Bat to play god— But then it's always this
way. From El Shaddai to Elohim, Yahweh to Yaakov,
Moshe to the son of man, that cult carpenter
who launched a thousand Elvises. Vaginal lips
to side slit to Jesus to Jesus—Mark's, Matthew's, Smith's.

From Thomas to Jefferson to the one called Koresh,
what we make we must make like Madonna, leaving
it all in the end, lighting for the tomb to be born.

DISCIPLINE & PUNISH

Wonder Woman crossing a stream clogged
with huge, long, and dangerous logs.

Wonder Woman bending back, sealing off
a bouquet of heavy howitzers.

Our princess of peace, her sororal sidekicks,
all tied to a pride of eager elephant trunks,

occupied with an octopus octaverate
of turgid tentacles, attacked

by animated ears of corn, bound and gagged
with a tethered leather mask, submerged

in a water tank, bound again, this time submarining
in a huge, long (and yes, dangerous) milk tank.

Wonder Woman wrapped wrist to foot by chain,
heal-hobbled by bomb, harried by eagle,

holding on by teeth alone to a rope
umbilicaled to her invisible plane.

Our heroine stripped, stretched, spanked, chained,
hotfooted, hogtied, roped in, roughed up, racked,

sacked, bivouacked, blindfolded, teased, tightly
trussed, handcuffed, electrified, infantilized,

crucified, negligeed . . . All images I'm afraid
I imagined. Everything Fredric Wertham

feared. He counted Wonder Woman too buff,
too into torture, handcuffs, and stuff.

Batman? Butt monkey. Everything else?
Too creepy to be believed. My own boss

had doubts. His son, another capital Gaines,
preferred *Crypt* to chick in superscript.

Even a soldier from the front lines once
asked, "Have you the same interest in fetters?"

Well, yes, of course, yes. I'm a man of letters:
WW, WMM, EC/DC, S & M.

Take another cover of that era, *World's Finest*
#7. Here, Supes, Bats, Robin ride astride steel

puns, three anti-aircraft guns. Typical
guys: big swatters, small flies. All, especially

the boy . . . well, no wonder it makes us wince.
The difference here is what's so prominent.

The simply dominant won't do. Power
isn't about doing. It's about screwing,

who screws who. Okay, too off the cuff, but
without wonder, power's not enough. *My* Wonder—

my egalitarian proletarian, my Amazon
who, with rope and bracelets and décolletage

came to teach us her Hajj, breech the deep divide
between dominance and inducement—

was made to fight the phallic, to counter bras
and wars, to infiltrate the enemy

through comic book stores, subvert the spectacles
testicles had made of the world. 1941.

Year of the red sun, advent of World War Two,
why not WW too? Brawn breeds less

law than lack, more black than blue.
So how *do* we stop the villain? Persuasion,

inducement, submission. Not what Dante built
his hell on. Love is the way to Paradise,

the way to circumcise what always seems to win,
the weapon that has made a slave of men.

WWII

Her cuffs crossing her for good or ill, Wonder
Woman is not all flash, not brash, but flesh
encased in power, virginity made invulnerable,
the most lush love locked away. She is the covered
uncovered, the shut which welcomes entry.
She is the bendable made unbreakable. She
is bone, wrist, muscle, mineral. Bracelet
against bullet, she is shield against all that might
invade, tear, rip the fabric of the light.
Bullets, missiles made of the metal of men,
never penetrate. They cannot, not because
she deflects (though she does), but because
she has become the tempered tool itself.
She *is* the metal casings she wears; she *is*
explosive, the power only barely contained
within. Such Wonder does not hide in darkness,
loom like doom, strike terror in cowardly
lots. She plots battle from her unseen plane,
herself, voluptuously visible. Yet, troth-
crossed, blood does spill. This is to be
expected. Her maker was human, probably
too. If I failed to animate the perfect
anima, my other, if creation got away,
grew confused, became what even Derrida
amused us deconstructing, if Wonder is
binary and, like thumbs, opposed, well,
Derrida himself disclosed his first emperor,
defrocked who he knew: Hyppolite. Yes,
there were two, like Diana Prince, like me, like you.

Doubled outside, doubled in. Half sinner, half
sin. Cinderella. Isis torn by identity crisis.
But not your typical fairy tale princess, all thumbs,
thimbles, spindles, and, spinning, grown old.
She'd hairpin that Stiltskin where he carries
his gold. Still . . . every bit woman, if warrior
crested. Amazon Tarzan, just double breasted.
XY *and* XX, yet more than sex, secretary,
faery flirt, skirt twirl, more than Gibson Girl,
Grimm trim, Andersen corsage, mere decoupage.
Our suppler doppelgänger. Wonder has to sunder
what she fights, and fighting, *become* other, both
Briar Rose and Briar's brother. Both Rapunzel
and what repels, both tower and tower's wells.
Boon? Bane? She climbs her own mane over turret
walls. She is all belle, all balls. She doesn't *need*
groom, costume, the return of another bloody shoe.
She is, as herself, WWI. As us? WWII.

THE DYNAMO AND THE VIRGIN

Adams said we are all products of lines
of force, patterns we may not even know.
Everything before Curie? Born of the dead
Virgin. Since then, the Dynamo. But Venus,
Eileithias, every earthen sleeve, each Eve
(Adams, even atoms notwithstanding) *remains*
force. Behind that force? Womb, the cave
from which we all crawl, still chained, blinking
in astonishment at the starry dynamo
of day. Day? Double to the night. Night?
Another cave, save above, not below.

So we move, from cave to cave, filling
each emptiness with what little light
we have, shadows casting shadows, dark
bodies beating transit between one lip's
eclipse and the next, leaving only coronas
the color of crime behind, pouring blood
into already bloody chambers, pulsing
from auricle to auricle, grail to grail,
like liquid released from some secret
chalice-stem hollow, drunk on our own
mad dash to be poisoned by what we love.

And behind that love? The absence that is
the heart, the pulse whose goal is always
to be empty, each beat proof against
the constancy of all that cannot remain
filled. Even caves give up their ghosts.

Even the grave. And behind the grave?
Me. The Creator. He who lived two lives,
cleaved to two wives. Am I so different
from you? Slave to forces that signify
that other lady's lover's nothing, I find it
hard to tell if what I've done, I've done alone.

From textbook to naughty novel, from Ivy
League to *Ladies' Home Journal,* polygraph
to pseudonym to superheroine, I've made
my living off others' inventions. The Virgin
for example. She was never mine, no, nor wholly
ours. Part history, part force, part matriarchal
marriage, part patriarch's divorce. I shaped
her from all I found around me, what was bound
to shape me. Elizabeth, Olive . . . Two loves
I moved between, two who, in helping shape
my offspring, my reach, let me lie with each.

From which cave, then, does wonder arrive?
From whence deception, conception, generation,
all that empty promise we can't explain? What lies
behind my most famous fabrication, behind me,
you, us, every accumulated myth? God I guess.
God-*dess.* We are Eve, more or less. We are
what follows. Serpent, penitent, sod. Both garden
and gardener's god. When we gain? Cain, able
to make absence into lives. Always outcast,
we are the questioner, the questioned who replies,
How do I love thee? Let me count the lies.

LIES

When a man lies, he kills some part of the world.
Merlin said that. But then, there was no Merlin,
no Arthur, no terrible table round as the mouth
of a grail. What then of the Grail itself? Could
it sleep, as some say, on the Isle of Man, at Rosslyn
Chapel, under a hill called Tor, Chalice Well
where the rocks bleed, or La Seo or Temple
Mount? Perhaps the cracks of the Caucasus,
two caves left from the spot they spiked Prometheus,
or Sarras—turn right, yes, now straight on—just south-
east of Jerusalem? Might it've been stolen,
kept, coveted, melted down, shilled for *wergild?*
So many cups, blades, vessels with pestles, flagons
with dragons. So many mights, so little will.

The thing about Christ's cup (no Christ, no cup),
is even Frost believed it a beginning place, just
that, an emptiness. A whence where we commence.
Childhood, directive. No, not even a story
on its own, but a tale more poured than told.
Raw material, smoldering, poised to fill a mold,
harden, be beaten, then filled itself, drunk, hence
emptied, only to fill that vessel filled already up
with hunger to be filled again. And so we glory
in the blood, always others', always ours. Lust
for what chatters through chest, chambers, lies
ever only *beyond* true beginning (God, guise),
knowing it is that—sea, river, flat—that once read
runs rampant in our veins, now leading, now led.

So is there any story, any tale we don't tell,
any beads of unborrowed blood? Is it in us,
to pound it out, new? What is true? *Where I steal
an idea, I leave my knife* . . . Michelangelo. *"Ode
On a Grecian Urn" is worth any number of little
old ladies* . . . Faulkner. Eliot? *Great writers steal.*
Nothing new. No under. No sun. Every lie,
who we are. Crystal, cave? All borrowed. All well
water tinged red, tainted by this flesh, zest,
this stain. And the world, what we coin real,
occluded always in the human eye. The mode
of seeing blotted out by the seen, being seen by.
So do we murder when we create, when we lie?
Merlin didn't begin to live until he had to die.

THE TEXT

They say Cheetah is retired now, seventy-one, living
in an old apes' home, learning the piano. Lassie?
All six of them long past retrieval. Lucy?
I imagine her signing "please," perhaps "take me
home," just before the poachers took her hands.
Even elephants, I've heard, leave flowers for the dead.

Signs. *Langue, parole,* signifier, signified . . .
We've been making shit up for at least a hundred
thousand years, believe we've surpassed
prairie dog dada, whale reel, the magnetic
appeal of bee polka, gone beyond the seismic,
foot-stomping bacchics of charismatic

pachyderms, and yet . . . Montauban, France.
A Protestant youth group comes to Mayrières
cave to help remove graffiti. Seventy hands, steel
wool, ancient, frightened bison. Calling themselves
Eclaireurs, "Those Who Show the Way," they
erase fifteen millennia by mistake. Don't forget

Chicago's Museum of Art. In "The Inventions
of the Monsters" we find a torso turning
to tortured furniture, a cherub churning
into clown, a rictal Madonna readying
butterfly vivisection. So many symbols,
so open to interpretation. But the only

one Dali said was no monster, his little blue
dog? Vanished. Egg based paint. Evaporation.
Ferdinand de Saussure? His only work,
the volume that revolutionized our theory
of sign, of meaning, his *Course in General
Linguistics,* could have been a recipe

for fish sticks. It certainly wasn't written
by him. Compiled post-mortem by students,
class notes. Then this: "San Francisco —
An abandoned parking barrier worshiped
as a shrine to the Hindu god of destruction
has been moved from Golden Gate . . .

It was dumped in the park several years ago
by a city crane operator. Last fall, Hindus
and New Agers discovered it and began
to worship at it. The city wanted it
removed, citing the need for separation
of church and state." What passes, then,

for meaning? What is text? Who makes it?
Which is more song? The sax solo Ron McNair
intended to play in space, or the bridge his body
made between the Challenger and its lonely last
rendezvous, the sea? Who sculpted the *Pietà*
at St. Peter's Basilica? For centuries it stood

with no signature. Not till some maniac,
hammer-handed, snuck in, cracked open Christ's
fist. There, in the broken hand of the broken
god, Michelangelo. Plain as the palm it crossed.
Some of these are stories, some even true.
Either way they remain. Take Orson Welles,

his voice the first voice of *The Shadow,*
he who could cloud men's minds. Nothing he said
about his life, nothing he revealed while living
told us anything that happened. But the myth,
so much bigger than him, lives on like that photo
of Whitman. You know the one, cardboard monarch

perched on his finger. No, even *The Crow,*
Bruce Lee's progeny, lingers. His son was dead, dead
as his dad before the film was finished. Bad bullets.
Stupid stunt. But they unearthed him from an early,
electric grave, made him jump and sprawl, made him
crawl again across the screen, completed what takes

it took and set him striding. Did I mention
he played a zombie? And what does this mean?
What did he want? What text knows the intent
of its father? What mother shapes exactly
the daughter she desires? What was Emily
thinking, sitting atop her Amherst tower,

writing poems to wrap hard candies in? What words
escaped the children she tossed them to? Maybe Einstein
had it right, bequeathed his brain to that science he loved.
But now his brain, diced like apple slices, boxed
in a box of Costa Brand apple cider, sits and sweats
behind a beer cooler in Wichita. D. H. Lawrence?

I hear for years his ashes receded in their urn.
Lost women, hungry for sons or lovers, kept
coming to his grave, measured out his death
with coffee spoons, mistook him for what little life
he'd given them. Author, authored, text, texture . . .
We live what lies we're given. Oscar Wilde

said a work of art's beauty "comes from the fact
that the author is what he is." But what is he?
Is she face or artifice? Where does poem end? Author?
Loving the author means leaving the text. Loving
the text means letting go. Alive, Wilde was imprisoned,
condemned. Today, to enter Westminster Abbey, first

the light must pass through glass they stained with him.

S/W
By S.

Clark. The Earth moved.

—WONDER WOMAN
The Dark Knight Strikes Again, 2002

SUPERMAN'S *OTHER* SECRET

It's strange, I suppose, to find myself spellbound,
in knots, as tongue-tied by her tossed locks
as the proverbial bad boy. Lassoed, trussed up
and forced to tell the truth under the influence
of that golden rope, doped. Lost in her main
means of defense, more shackled than she
by her mettle, those magic manacles. Unable
to dodge the bullets that, heartward, seem to hum.
Mostly, she avoids them. I just let them come.

I'm supposed to be taken, I know. Good guy,
steady as the morning star, faithful as that apple
pie Lois sometimes bakes me, a *fine* example.
But then there's two of me, as many (more?) of her.
Smart, savvy, strong enough to beat all she can't
bear. As beautiful as any stag she might have done
in, outrun, caught, antlers askance, standing
in the still. Goddess? Okay, demi-, but born to shame
that lack of choice, Paradise, from which she sprang.

Woman of steel, mistress of the upper air,
she knows how each of us is always already
falling. Alone with her, I seem to understand
earth, its breath, better, the orgasm of ozone
that rushes out when she describes her own
flight. Even sitting—stratus, nimbostratus,
talking—I've watched her turn into it, dive,
ride it the way she does her stories, worries, cares.
The shape of the wind. What her world wears.

Me, I just point and leap, but not with her.
Some days I fear that I'm invisible as the plane
she doesn't need, a spectacle in a suit, uptight,
upright, perhaps *too*. Or that, though our colors clash
the same, hers cut closer to the breast. Even weaknesses . . .
I fear mine are mine alone. No recurring villains,
no green rocks, a decided lack of chains. And though
we both could leap this difference, in fact much less,
there is a yaw yet, deep as regret, from farmboy to finesse.

SUPERMAN, ON WONDER WOMAN

Her brow is bronze, her breast is gold,
upon her mons the stars of old
collect as if to start the sky
again, at join of thigh and thigh.

The eagle that between her breasts
withholds its talons, turns and nests,
must know it is no simple *S,*
that symbols such as it caress

the liminal, the great divide
between the hunt and hunter's hide,
it stands, as she, for dream foresworn,
King Edwin's bird from storm to storm

aflight within the Mead Hall's warmth,
both soul and sparrow, death and hearth.
It's Keats' nightingale *and* Keats,
lark for Shelley, arc for Yeats,

it's albatross and darkling thrush,
Leda's lover, Hopkins' hush
that settles on the world and broods,
the final shape for Dante's moods,

both dove and doom for T.S.E.,
for Pound, a cuckoo, same as he,
for Wordsworth, immortality,
for Freud, a nightmare of H.D.,

for Philomel, a tongue to speak,
for those who bring us fire, beak.
Dickinson took the beast apart,
found it silent after art.

Sexton let it take her eyes,
and Plath? The phoenix never dies.
O'Connor's peacocks, Nin's nine birds,
Faulkner's follies, words, words, words.

Roc or rooster, bat or squirrel,
stripling hero, little girl,
from Chauvet's walls to outback rock,
from grunt to sign to song to talk

to page to book to magazine
to celluloid to cathode screen,
from Horus to *The Hawkman,* kitsch,
from Crimson Avenger to Scarlet Witch,

the figure that surmounts her skirt,
beats its wings beneath her shirt,
rises from her girdled waist,
sets her apart from the commonplace,

is one part shield, one boustier,
one image of the life that clay
took on when Hippolyte fed
that lifeless lump with heart that bled

for all of us, and bleeds there still.
Wonder Woman, whip and will.

W.W.F.

The biggest struggles don't come in tights.
It's not like it is on TV, facing the Hulk
Hogans of the world, the Undertakers,
the Rowdy Pipers. It's not Spiderman
crossing Crusher; Banner, the Abomination.
Not even Clark Kent and Cassius Clay, alien
versus Ali under some synthetic red sun. No,
nor the Claw or Bone Saw, the Giant, Rock, Stone
Cold, all those long locked brothers. We *do* know
the ring, the crowd sound. Can count, on the ropes,
the exact number of enemies at our backs.
But when that hand reaches in from outside,
slaps our sleeve to let us know we're not alone,
when the melee ensues, bodies piling up
until we can't distinguish friend from fiend,
foe from phony, when the referee goes down
and the chairs begin to fly, tables upended,
all pretensions dropped, lines forgotten, fake
physics made suddenly very real, even then,
each dream teaming of masks (Sandman
vs. Slaughter; The Body, The Spirit) breaks down.

Say, for example, you love two women. One,
a writer. The other, all your friends claim, alive.
The former, her parents called Lois Lane long before
she came to this state, learned the lingo, turned
toward the planet you share for worship. You fell
first for her stories, for the luster of each lush
word, glottal glory, resolved backstory, her perfect

agreement, but you've been with her long enough
now to know better. Nights out with the uptown
crew, nights *in* with computer, reams, dreams,
a dozen dirtied wine stems. Small piles of skin
picked from her ear till it bleeds, the tub she keeps
falling into, the nightmares—*No, please no*—the candle
left burning that nearly . . . Then, one night, the scream
when she saw you, yet didn't. And no one but you
suspects, not even her. The secrets of identity.
The stories we tell. What exits us must always
also enter. Incubus, Oedipus, Judas
kiss. What have these to do with empty bottles
hidden in the backs of cabinets? Words
know nothing of the mouths that shape them.

So what words are left for you who wants
to leave? Chickenshit? Judas, you've already
used and probably will again. It's not like you
planned any of this, yet here in the thick of battle
the gloves and capes and masks are off, and she
who would have been isn't anymore. An Amazon
stands in the other corner, someone you never saw
entering the ring. And what now? Abandon
your partner, throw in the towel, tired of holding back
her hair? Or is this too-ready recrimination?
Did you already know what you'd planned when last
you left her, flying off to wrestle reptiles
in your head? All you know is this: This
woman, this new figure is, even now, too fitting
for your own. You both have hidden things, terrible
things, have burned and been burned, but neither wants
to keep those secrets alone. She, your *other* love,
once plummeted from plane into power, got caught
in the current, volts vaulting her system one organ

at a time, but electric burns are not like any
other. They follow no preordained path.

Moving like life itself through the body,
they mark you. They mark her. They are obvious
and they are beautiful and—even in her robes,
one ringlet shining against skin against scar—
they move you like she moves you, passing through
your body one wonder at a time. So, Judas,
you must choose. You will watch Lois crumble
and cry and beg, and you (you already know this),
you will leave. You will turn from her and deny
and deny and, finally, at cock crow, hope
that what you do will make her hate you. Then,
when you have left libation behind, left word
for wisdom, reporter for typist, flesh for spirit
and spirit once more for she who is, more fully
flesh... Then, only then, will you also leave costume
for consummation, embrace all you find
in the ring, let go the little battles and learn to love
the fire that comes with this new sun, this scarlet
skald, herself a herald of Hera's word, the only flame
you were meant to fight, what no candle left
lit could burn, what no gilt, no grudge could match.

W.W.J.D.

"This is my body," said the man,
and no one heard above the din
of plate and pot and serving pan

save the one who knew the sin
of lying better than his master,
knew true teaching could begin

only when at last catastr-
ophe'd muddied their sandals some.
A parable's fast, disaster's faster.

Stale bread? Bad wine? Quite frankly none
of these would bring an acolyte
to give himself for *anyone.*

Jor-El, my father, sacrificed
himself, his world, and all he loved,
betrayed it, like that other, thrice.

He knew why Krypton's mantle moved,
its seashelves sinking, orbit shot.
His every theory, tested, proved.

Yet no one guessed but him. His lot
was silence as he turned away
to save his son, and, through me, not

a minor portion of each day
our race had served beneath our sun,
our only Rao, which Dad's survey

had shown would bleed, begin to run,
at long last blast itself, like me,
out into void, Rao's will be done.

On the one hand, host, the other, holy.
The one, the other's faith and fear.
It's not the *begotten* but the *only*

part of *son* that matters here.
So, yes, each J. gave up stuff, shed
some shell to show what should cohere.

But *did* he do right? *Should* he have fled?
We're told, with rope, one made it good.
I think, though, like his master did,

he got hung up on *would.*

SEVERAL STORIES, SINGLE BOUND

I. SMALLVILLE

As if where we begin could be anything
but everything. Small? No, I remember
cotton and corn and milo, beans and sunflowers,
fields stretching across that skeleton of sky
taut and vast and rich with a midsummer
sheen that seemed to glow from both sides
of the horizon. Here, they grew their religion
big as their pumpkins. Hundred pound gods,
churches plump as prize steers, sermons
that could feed a multitude. And drive-ins.
Screens plastered like runways against the night,
blotting out stars, each flat canvas expanse
only making those that eked the edges
all the brighter. Bread belly, Bible basket, single

stories. It was here I first found love. Harvesting.
She was country, I was uncool, and December
came to unspool that year with meteor showers
and she and I beneath them, naked as July
in her parents' loft—half light, half lumber.
Only *after* did it seem small. So love elides...
No, love simply leads . . . away. The contagion,
though, was the same. Now everything (Pa's
values, Ma's meddling, even the soft ermine
of Lana's legs, what brought me to the horns
of my dilemma) grew suspect. It wasn't right.
Of *course* we can't blame dancer for the dance,

but suddenly farm and family, all the hedges
I'd grown up growing behind, seemed too green, L.

L. Bean, simple, slight. My need, new sight, called first for haze.
This was just lost, not star-crossed. It takes more than corn to amaze.

II. ATLANTIS

Just what do we leave lying when we leap?
What remains prone, undaunted, vaunted, asleep?
Each building, what we vault, is made from stories,
tales that stretch down as deep as they may rise.
The tale I left Lana for was deep indeed, perhaps
different, perhaps not. Lori Lemaris,
second set of double Ls, second layer
of life's love's hells, was a mermaid, mostly,
as lean and lovely as the life she led. Half
flipper, half honey, she drew me down to crest
like kraken over berm, under isotherm into all
those hollows I didn't know before, the absence
we must hold to scaffold presence on. And being
only half here, heir to only one part air,

she taught what it means to breathe, breathe deep,
how the lungs call out for what they can't keep
the way waves reclaimed her city, whole histories,
her, the way Ekman spiral and Coriolis
force conspire to create current, the lapse
and the reprise that lie beneath each tug, each urge
for more than what we have. *Her* only prayer
was always for ever less, for nothing costly,
an ocean vent, a patch of blue. But *not* to have,
this costs too. Letting go desire, what's repressed,

scaling down to nothing but the next sea wall,
the next handful of krill. Some part of us resents
not having anything to leave. Me? I started seeing,
yes, but saw below the sea she wasn't there.

Jor-El, Lara, Lana, Lori, even dear damned Lex . . . I found ways
of leaping what I couldn't be—law, love, loss. All *L*s I left for praise.

III. METROPOLIS

If love is built on stories, then lovers must be
condemned to build again. What we leave
behind? All those cables and portals and panes?
Shadows, whole suburbs of souls, metropoles
of abandon. Spires like twisted, frozen fire,
fetters, lonely letters. *L*s, double *L*s, like stripped
flowers or twin towers. My own home town? Two
sets of two. So why, particularly, *L?* Any letter,
say I, would do, but *L, an* ell is an extension
set at right angles to a building, a wing, annex.
An el? A train. I can jump one, outrun the other.
No, the other, the *else,* is precisely whom I can't.
Lang, Lemaris, Luthor, none were the last. Lois
Lane, though, another double, another vast

catacomb of glass, lush life to leap, story
to keep alive only in leaving . . . She, I believed,
would last, long past that narrative demesne
of tales too worth getting lost in, the shoals
of souls' sea-change, the bed of dead desire.
But she drank, whimpered like the whipped
in her sleep, carried scars from sources few
reporters would reveal. Some days were better,

didn't need to save her, avoid evil invention.
But no power can protect the one who panics,
stays yet flies, makes the simple sins of lovers'
lives into need, invents reason to seize, to sell it slant,
rationalize, be one at home, elsewhere, otherwise.
Need spins stories to lies, less. But even void has mass.

All truths are the same. With mass comes gravity, sad beauty, that
    bizarro craze
to bring back down what lifts us up. Each planet turns, unearthed
    urns, cracked glaze.

IV. THEMYSCIRA

Of all the cities, lives, loves I've left for good,
only one still stands beyond the power of man
for ruin. The stories we construct eventually
crumble; this is given. But after the inevitable
fall, after the wind and smoke have cleared, after
the smell of the dead has left us in its wake,
after doomsday, after hero, long after ground
zero, after you and I have failed to reconvene
any semblance of what passes for civilized,
there will always be one city, one nation not fraught
with predation or pity, one island that still lies
outside imagination. I call her Paradise.
Here, at last I've entered, found my final fortress keep,
a tower, bower, citadel, a love I dare not leap.

She is not architrave raised to praise maidenhood,
not bullet turret for some patriarchal plan.
Not portico or pavilion, garrison or galley,
mere addition. Not fault's vault, nor rule's vestibule,

no structure supported lightly. No amber chamber,
no battlement to storm, and during storming, take.
Never arch or abutment only, bas relief or round.
She is more than ziggurat, bachelor flat, temple, scene.
She is, as is her island, a reservoir of real realized,
sight unparalyzed, all the wonder I have sought.
Some say her allure is a long lasso, longer thighs,
perhaps risk, the statuesque, the power to paralyze
with looks. Regardless, she is goddess, girdle of the deep.
Her arms are my island. Her shackles, where I sleep.

Stories bound by leaps, loss embossed by lies. All we've built, our
    model guilt, bottled by a phrase.
Love, that city in a bottle (in all candor, us), *is* else, is pulse, our
    American dream. Our Amazon daze.

A MODEST PROPOSAL

I.

So what do you do, caught now, supposed to catch?
What, when in your wonder, you've finally met your match?

Sweep her to the top of some tall building? Take a chance
she might not share your view, might chuckle, worse, wince

when, knuckling to one knee you find your tongue
capricious as your cape, buffeted by the wind her long

locks languidly molest, tangled in the tempest of her eyes?
What *should* one say, one who's made a life of lies?

What, to she who's spent hers *denying* what denies,
hog-tying all who'd hobble honor? Turncoats, spies.

Is this, you must ask, is this the one? Are you, well,
done flitting from city to city, from this small vil-

lage to that, from dust bowl to metropol to the crude
Fortress you've crafted of ice and loss? Can you toss solitude?

You know she's known flyboys before, at least one
she tried to save. Will you be that bold, that brave? Some

or none of this will bind your mind as you finally crash
into them, your words, all you have to offer: First, *ash,*

offer her ash, the end of who you were alone;
next, *blood,* since, up till now you might have well been stone;

then, *lightning*—you know you'll have to jolt her to the bone;
last, *loam,* remembering how you'll need to seed the home

for which you paid high price, how, at least once, maybe twice,
at beginnings other than this, you both lost Paradise.

II.

So, ash, blood, lightning, loam. Remember these, these and foam
brought Aphrodite herself to life. Promise everything. Assume

strife. Assume love. Assume this diamond you made for now,
what you held in your hand and squeezed, this vow,

this tiny reflection of her, her strength, her Goddesshood,
her life, its length, your life together, shant, should,

will, won't, important, moot, *all* of you, your will, your suit,
all you own, ever sought, dog, cat, super, not,

family now, family then, battered, bothered, bottled
kin, fragments reflected across the divide, that addled

space where secrets hide, blow like stellar wind between
dead planets no one's ever seen, islands where the gusts careen

above the place where planes are lost, you, she, stories
tossed, every building, every spire, every worry,

each desire, sister saved from crashing craft,
a son from another life . . . oh, that other raft . . .

all you imagine, all you'll share, love of flight,
the diving dare, dashing rush, ash, lust, light . . .

Well, assume that this diamond you made for now,
what you hold in your hand and squeeze, this vow,

assume what it means, the future, this mix
of dimensions far fairer than Mxyzptlk's,

this promise you make, this thing you ask,
is, at its least, your greatest task.

LAST WORDS ON WONDER

So, I wonder at the wonder of my Wonder.
I suppose you think I'm repeating myself
already, but then none of this was ever
only for you. Who are you? A reader?
Aren't I? When I say *I wonder* aren't I,
by definition, begging the question, tapping
into *perhaps* or, otherwise, *reflection?*

Aren't I, if I'm not satisfied with *is,*
always interrogating *might?* Super,
maybe I'll just keep this up then, maybe
it all means too much *not* to play with puns,
our selves, others', myths we mulch from words,
what we're made of. So much we need
to get off our chests, me especially.

Take this *S.* It could've easily been *W*
or, say, some bat, bolt, lantern, four, maybe *R* or
Fe, the egghead name for iron. But none
of it would be me, not that, nor what you see.
And what, I wonder, does that mean for E
= mc, squared roots, round worlds, flat lines
in an Alabama abortion clinic?

Hey, you say, there it is again, geek think:
If we only lived like characters in comic
books. If only our colors were true,
three-part separation. If thoughts showed up
above heads in scalloped balloons. If maybe

motive made appearance in our names, the more
alluring and alliterative the better . . .

I could echo Eco who sees me as subject
to a cycle, to every plot that can't end,
my acts amply empty compared to what
must be possible, for me. Eco makes more
of this than what's at first apparent, fosters
distrust for my morals (Man of Steal?). I'd say
the same for myself, if it weren't for the fact . . .

Well, if we were just . . . I don't know, if we were just
more than that *less* we assume from such stories.
We repeat ourselves. A hero is a hero,
some say. Why get carried away? But am I
not to trust Jesus just because he smacks too much
of Odysseus, or Isis after Saturday
cartoons? How about symbols themselves, me?

Aren't we all, by comparison, drawn a little
bit flat? We wonder. We guess. Repeat after me,
does that make us more comic or less?

About the Author

BRYAN D. DIETRICH is the author of a book-length study on comics, *Wonder Woman Unbound*, and six books of poems, *Krypton Nights* (published previously by Zoo Press), *Universal Monsters, Love Craft, Prime Directive, The Assumption*, and *The Monstrance*. He is also co-editor of *Drawn to Marvel*, an anthology of superhero poetry.

He has published poems in *The New Yorker, The Nation, Poetry, Ploughshares, Prairie Schooner, The Paris Review, Harvard Review, The Yale Review, Shenandoah, Open City, Asimov's Science Fiction, Witness, Weird Tales*, and many other journals.

Having won *The Paris Review* Poetry Prize, a "Discovery"/*The Nation* Award, a Writers at Work Fellowship, the *Isotope* Editors' Prize, an *Asimov's* Reader's Choice Award, and the Eve of St. Agnes Prize, Dietrich is also a five-time finalist for the Yale Younger Poets Series and has been nominated multiple times for both the Pushcart and the Pulitzer.

Dietrich is currently Professor of English and Chair of the Division of Arts and Letters at Newman University in Wichita, Kansas.